RUGBY LE
in the 'Fifties

C000155095

RUGBY LEAGUE JOURNAL
PUBLISHING

Volume Three in the 'Rugby League Journal History Series'

This book is dedicated to every schoolboy's hero of the 'Fifties

First published in Great Britain in 2012 by
Rugby League Journal Publishing
P.O.Box 22, Egremont, Cumbria, CA23 3WA

ISBN 978-09548355-7-6

Written, edited and designed by Harry Edgar
Marketing and promotion by Ruth Edgar
Printed by The Firpress Group Limited

Front cover pictures:
Main picture: Billy Boston playing for Great Britain on the 1954 tour.
Inset pictures: Dave Valentine, Lewis Jones and Willie Horne.
Frontispiece picture:
British forwards Nat Silcock and Jack Wilkinson playing in Australia in 1954.

RUGBY LEAGUE JOURNAL
PUBLISHING

P.O. Box 22, Egremont, Cumbria, CA23 3WA
E-Mail: rugbyleague.journal@sky.com   Telephone: 01946 811005
www.rugbyleaguejournal.net

Contents

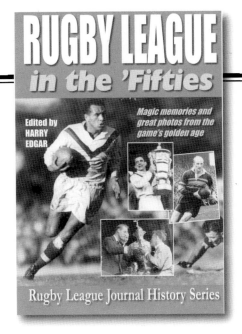

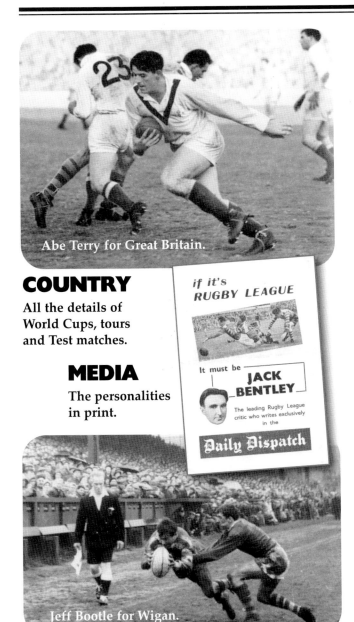

Abe Terry for Great Britain.

COUNTRY

All the details of
World Cups, tours
and Test matches.

MEDIA

The personalities
in print.

if it's
RUGBY LEAGUE

It must be — **JACK BENTLEY**

The leading Rugby League
critic who writes exclusively
in the

Daily Dispatch

Jeff Bootle for Wigan.

CLUB Details of the Cups and Championships.

*The Publishers would like to thank all friends who assist
"Rugby League Journal" and whose loan of valuable
photographs and items of memorabilia have helped in the
compilation of this book. Our thanks also to all the
photographers whose skills have provided so many fine
images - with so many old pictures from private collec-
tions it is often difficult to ascertain their origins, thus
there has been no intention to breach anybody's copyright.
The first person articles attributed to the trio of legendary
international captains (all now sadly deceased) - Dave
Valentine, Alan Prescott and Puig-Aubert - have been
compiled from previously published articles by them and,
in some cases, personal converstaions with the Editor.*

Among the galaxy of star players who lit up the 1950s, none was more brilliant throughout the decade than Warrington's flying winger Brian Bevan, pictured *(above)* playing against Halifax in the 1954 Challenge Cup Final at Wembley. Bevan was the most unlikely looking of rugby superstars, but the fans flocked to see him - not just at Wilderspool, but throughout the Rugby League grounds of the north of England. The man who became the game's all-time world record try-scorer, topped the League lists in three seasons during the 1950s, and finished outside of the game's top five try-scorers only once. As an Australian playing in England, Bevan was also a mainstay of the famous Other Nationalities team.

Introduction

Welcome to the third book in our "Rugby League Journal History Series" as we take you back to the 1950s. Our publishing motto remains the same as with our previous volumes - more nostalgia for the older generation to enjoy, and another chance to record some of the game's history for future generations to learn from. It is always our hope that by making available in print a collection of memorabilia and so many wonderful old photographs, we might stimulate a new interest among younger fans in studying Rugby League's past and respecting its heritage.

That was always the case for me as far as the 'fifties were concerned. I only just caught the end of the decade in the flesh, watching my first Rugby League match as a child in 1959, but I knew all about the great names and famous events which had gone before in stories handed down by my father, along with the treasure trove of old programmes and newspaper cuttings he kept in a shoebox. That planted the seed of interest in me for the game, and especially its presentation via the printed word, and I had an excellent teacher in my father. The 'fifties were his era, as he avidly followed the fortunes

of Rugby League and the Workington Town and Barrow clubs in particular, largely because his idols were Gus Risman and Willie Horne. Because of that, I grew up to hold sportsmen like Gus and Willie in awe, although I never had the privilege of seeing them play, and it was the same for other names my father used to tell me about in such reverential terms: Ernest Ward, Joe Egan, Ken Gee, Martin Ryan, Johnny Lawrenson, Billy Ivison, Jimmy Ledgard, Tony Paskins, Brian Bevan, Jimmy Lewthwaite and an Australian called Clive Churchill.

Whilst Borough Park and Craven Park were my father's favourite haunts as the places where he watched his local heroes every Saturday afternoon, he would also travel further afield to watch big matches at major venues like Wigan's Central Park and Maine Road, Manchester. And he took great

(Pictured) **Gus Risman with the Cup at Wembley in 1952. Gus and Barrow's Willie Horne were held in awe.**

delight in telling me the tale of when the French team Marseille came to play Workington at Borough Park, and about the crazy little scrum-half they had called Jean Dop. It was with particular delight that, many years later, I became friends with the very same Jean Dop as he enthralled me with stories from his two tours to Australia in 1951 and '55. As time passed, I got to know many similar people who played such a part in Rugby League in the 'Fifties, shaping the history of the game which we now look back on so fondly in the pages of this book.

I hope this volume will bring readers as much pleasure in looking at it as it gives me in compiling it. For those who were there in the 'Fifites, I hope the memories will be happy ones. And for those involved in the modern game of Rugby League today, I hope they might give some thought to a saying often quoted by Harry Bath, who played a pivotal part throughout the 1950s first at Warrington and then back home in Australia with St.George. Harry would say: "Those who drink the water, should remember the people who dug the well." And certainly those people who made Rugby League what it was in the 'Fifties have left a wonderful legacy to all future generations, as you will see in the pages that follow ...

HARRY EDGAR (Editor "Rugby League Journal")

You've never had it so good

(Above)
Bob Coverdale in possession against the French pack during the 1954 World Cup match at Toulouse. The British player in support is York's Basil Watts. This was the first Rugby League international to be played in the new Toulouse stadium, known as a "mini-Wembley," and drew a French record crowd of 37,471 paying spectators. The success of France in the 'Fifties, and their promotion of the World Cup, had much to do with the vibrancy of the international game.

It was a quote from the soon-to-be Prime Minister, Harold McMillan, in 1957 which came to represent much of the decade of the 'Fifties. When Mr. McMillan said *"Most of our people have never had it so good ..."* he was referring to a Britain which had recovered from post-war austerity and was enjoying a time of full employment. People's lives were changing with the growing popularity of television and availability of motor cars, and there was much about Rugby League in the 1950s to suggest the game had never had it so good.

Perhaps life for the working people of the industrial towns of Lancashire, Yorkshire and Cumberland might not have been quite as sweet as Harold McMillan was envisaging, and certainly Rugby League clubs at the lower end of the scale still had plenty of problems to ovecome to keep their financial heads above water, but from a big picture point of view the sport was full of optimism and ambition. The lead was set by having a vibrant international programme of tours and Test matches. In Australia, the public was able to see visiting international teams in every single year of the 'Fifties; whilst in Europe a closely fought international championship, which prospered in the early years of the decade, eventually was overtaken by an annual Test series between Great Britain and France. In addition, Europe hosted five major tours from Australasia during the 1950s, with the icing on the cake the establishment of the World Cup in 1954. Rugby League was so far ahead of other sports in this respect, and with the growth of air-travel the sky appeared to be the limit. The 'Fifties also saw the game make bold attempts to widen its international horizons; first with the establishment of a Welsh League, then attempts to promote the game in America with the infamous All Stars tours of 1953 followed by Australia playing New Zealand in California on their way home from the 1954 World Cup, and various links with Italy which saw the decade close with the establishment of a fully-fledged Italian League of over 20 clubs in two divisions. In addition, the game was also played in Yugoslavia, largely encouraged by the French and Italians, and the 1957 World Cup teams of Britain and France played promotional games in South Africa.

Hindsight tells us that Rugby League's fatal problem was in not being able to maintain any of these initiatives, for a variety of reasons which are for historians to explain. But all that activity on the international front was underpinned in Britain by a domestic League in which all clubs were together in one big division, and all were treated as equal partners. With only one or two exceptions among the perennial strugglers, every club set out at the start of each season confident it could challenge for honours, whilst at the same time all could produce players for the international team. The "holy grail" was to achieve a top-four place and challenge for the Championship, but it was the knockout cups which were most eagerly anticipated - the County Cups in the first part of each season and then the Challenge Cup after Christmas. Some huge crowds were generated for Challenge Cup ties, especially the semi-finals when teams were just one game away from their dream of walking out at Wembley, and a pinnacle was reached on a memorable night at Odsal in 1954 when over 102,000 were crammed in to watch a replay of the Final.

Optimism abounded with the creation of new clubs at Doncaster and Blackpool, and the building of a brand new ground by Workington Town, whilst clubs were financially confident enough to spend big money on transfer-fees and the recruitment of players from Rugby Union. But not everybody in Rugby League was able to share Harold McMillan's view of things - Cardiff lasted only one season as a senior club and was a financial disaster for the Northern Rugby League; Doncaster, after a tremendously positive debut season, soon ran into financial problems; and Belle Vue Rangers were forced to pull out of the League in 1955 when they couldn't find a suitable ground, leaving the game's presence in Manchester severely diminished. But for most Rugby League players, picking up winning money that was often more than they earned in a whole week in their day jobs - making them better off than many "full time " soccer players - truly they had never had it so good.

(Above)
Not such a good moment for Ron Ryder, the Warrington centre, as he is helped from the field by assistant-trainer Griff Jenkins after playing a big part in the Wire's 1950 Cup semi-final win over Leeds in front of 70,198 people at Odsal. Ryder was injured with concussion 12 minutes from the end, but recovered well from his distress. Ryder would go on to play in Great Britain's Ashes winning team in 1952, and later be the new Blackpool Borough club's first player-coach in 1954. As for Griff Jenkins, he became one of the top coaching figures of the 'fifties as he took charge of the Oldham team which was one of the decade's outstanding outfits, becoming Champions in 1957.

Rock and roll is here to stay

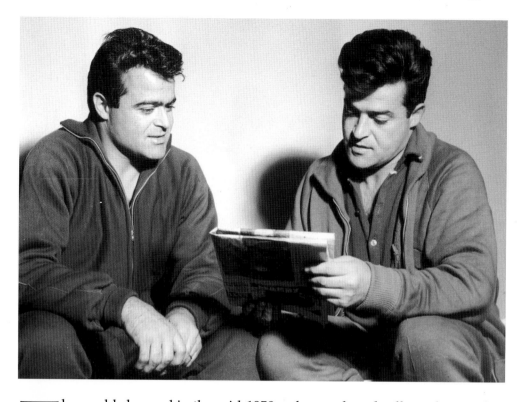

(Right)
Who needs the Everly brothers when you can have Gilbert and Rene Benausse. The French brothers both played for the mighty Carcassonne club and were internationals for France. But could they also sing harmony like Don and Phil? French fans in the 1950s would tell you there was nothing that Gilbert Benausse couldn't do as he took over the mantle from Puig-Aubert as France's greatest player.

(Above)
A young Elvis Presley in 1955. His influence was felt all the way from Memphis to Mirfield as the word "teenager" entered the English language and Rugby League was never the same.

The world changed in the mid-1950s when rock and roll was born. After Bill Haley and his Comets has rocked around the clock and a young singer called Elvis Presley from Memphis shot to fame, life was never going to be the same. Teenagers were invented, and suddenly everything looked different for the younger generation. Young men who played Rugby League were no different, as hairstyles and attitudes changed. When the 1956 Kangaroo touring team played Test matches in England, they complained about the noise coming from the opposing dressing room as, apparently, Geoff Gunney played the latest rock and roll records - just how Geoff had managed to get a gramophone player into the dressing room, nobody knows.

The 1958 Great Britain touring team were definitely the first of the rock n' roll era, such were the changes that had taken place since the previous tour in 1954. With Vinty Karalius sporting his teddy-boy quiff, Alex Murphy his brylcream and Dick Huddart's hobby listed in the pen-pictures as "collecting gramophone records," the Aussies soon realised these boys were a bit different to the staid fellows from the Mother Country they had welcomed on previous tours. Perhaps it was no surprise that on the 1958 tour there was much unrest, and almost a mutiny, as the manager "Barney" Manson and coach Jim Brough found it impossible to bridge the huge generation gap between themselves and the players.

And even less surprising that the players saw as their saviour the team manager Tom Mitchell, a cosmopolitan character with a beatnik-style beard, who wore suede shoes, ran around with the players wearing shorts, and thought nothing of going water-skiing in Sydney harbour in the week of a Test match. Tom was one of Rugby League's most progressive officials, and was the driving force behind the creation of Workington Town's new ground at Derwent Park. As a prominent member of the Rugby League Council, he often found himself at odds with the secretary, Bill Fallowfield, who was also - like Mitchell - a Cambridge graduate and a man eager to have the game rise

1954

1958

(*Left*)
Pictures which show how appearances had changed in the years between the 1954 and 1958 Lions tours. The top group of British players in Australia in 1954 look like mature businessmen and some even had their gaberdine macs with them, whilst the group below, in 1958, show this was the first tour of the rock n' roll age with players in tee-shirts and American-style checked shirts bought from the Army surplus store. Along with Vinty's teddy-boy quiff and the sight of manager Tom Mitchell cavorting in shorts, you can see why poor old "Barney" Manson didn't know what was happening and thought all discipline was going out of the window.

above the parochialism which bedevilled it in so many ways. Fallowfield was an internationalist, who championed the attempted development of the game in Wales, Italy and South Africa, and always ensured a close relationship of co-operation with the French. He also quickly recognised the need to embrace television, rather than obstruct it, although Rugby League became more and more embroiled in arguments about how to use it as the new medium's influence continued to grow as the 'fifties progressed. The changes brought about in the second half of the decade were dramatic - the players on the 1958 tour would never have dreamt of setting off for Australia wearing heavy gaberdine raincoats as many of their 1950 and 1954 counterparts did - but even they could not "out fashion" the charismatic French manager Antoine Blain as he set off for the 1951 tour on a blazing hot day at Marseille airport wearing a duffle-coat, which he proceeded to wear throughout his entire journey around Australia and New Zealand.

(*Above*)
Oysters for lunch for Mick Martyn and Brian McTigue during the 1958 tour to Australia. But not as good as the ones they got in the Leigh and Wigan markets.

After being held by the British for fully thirty years, the Ashes were finally won by Australia in 1950 amid joyous scenes among the Aussies at the Sydney Cricket Ground. Ernest Ward's Lions had been unable to overcome the freakish quagmire conditions and the vagaries of Australian refereeing, and lost the Test series 2-1. Ward's 1950 Lions were the last British touring team to travel down-under by boat, which meant clubs would no longer have to worry about losing star players for their big finals at the end of the season. Attempts had been made to stage the 1950 Challenge Cup Final earlier than its usual date in May, but they proved unsuccessful, so as the tourists set sail to Australia on 20th April, none of them were able to play at Wembley. This meant Warrington had to play the Cup Final without their international forwards Jim Featherstone and Bob Ryan, whilst Widnes were missing Fred Higgins and Dan Naughton. There were no surprises, as Warrington won comfortably 19-nil.

(Above)
The Wigan team at Maine Road, minus their eight Great Britain tourists and captained by Cec Mountford, before famously beating Huddersfield in the Championship Final of 1950. It crowned a great season for Wigan, who were unbeaten at Central Park.

However, in the Championship Final at Maine Road seven days later, the loss of a record eight players away on tour, meant Wigan lined up against the star-studded Huddersfield outfit as rank outsiders. But Wigan's "A" teamers rose to the occasion magnificently to win a record seventh Championship title. Wigan had finished top of the Northern Rugby League, six points clear of second-placed Huddersfield, but without their eight tourists had, ominously, been held to a draw by Halifax at Central Park in the top-four play-off, only for the Wigan "reserves" to win a replay at Thrum Hall 18-2. Remarkably, the cosmopolitan Huddersfield side did not have a single player in the Lions touring team, and they had overcome third-placed Swinton 9-nil at Fartown in the top-four play-off.

Under the guidance of Bill Fallowfield, the secretary of the Rugby League and the International Board which had been founded in 1948, it was a time of great opitmism and ambition in the game. Its coaching scheme was fully up and running, and much missionary work was taking place to spread Rugby League's horizons, notably in the London area where the Southern Amateur Rugby League had been formed with Mr. J. W. Hogg as its organiser. In 1950 Mr. Hogg and his southern colleagues became the subject of much media attention when they ran into the problems of anti-League prejudice which tried to stop servicemen play-

---

Elsewhere in the world of sport in 1950

* England enter the soccer World Cup for the first time, but suffer an inglorious shock 1-0 defeat to the U.S.A. in Belo Horizonte, Brazil.
*The Scotland football team are beaten at home for the first time by a foreign nation when they lose 1-0 to Austria in December.
*South African Bobby Locke wins the British Open Golf Championship for the second successive year.
*The inaugural Formula One drivers world championship is won by Italian Giuseppe Farina driving an Alfa Romeo, after a seven race series.

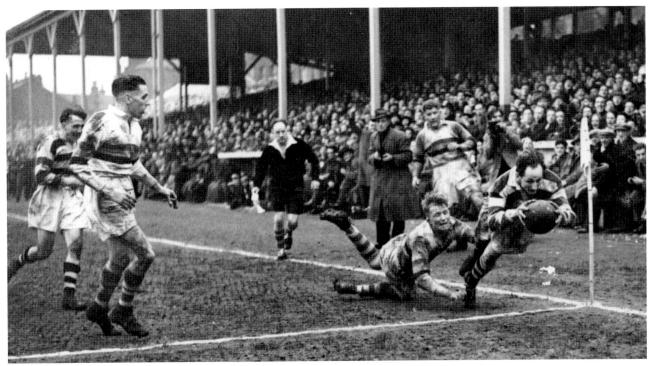

ing the 13-aside game as amateurs. Meanwhile a Welsh League was up and running with as many as ten teams, two of which - Cardiff and Llanelly - had ambitions of joining the Northern Rugby League. Cardiff played Salford in the 1950 Challenge Cup, losing 15-10 in the first leg of the tie in Wales and then 20-5 in the return leg at the Willows. Visitors from further afield arrived in August 1950, when an Italian team played a six match tour.

Many clubs were unhappy that the international transfers ban was in place, denying them the opportunity of signing ready made Rugby League stars from Australia, and in the summer of 1950 Bradford Northern's ambitious chairman, Mr. Harry Hornby, embarked on a remarkable recruitment mission by flying to New Zealand and coming back with five Rugby Union players at a reported cost of £10,000 - among them All Black winger Jack McLean who proved to be a prolific try scorer.

(Above) **Tommy Sale dives over to score for Widnes in their 8-nil 1950 Challenge Cup semi-final win over**

TOP TEN

1949-50
TRIES
57 B. Nordgren (Wigan)
46 L. Cooper (Huddersfield)
36 A. Daniels (Halifax)
34 W. Blan (Wigan)
33 B. Bevan (Warrington)
32 R. Cracknell (Huddersfield)
31 J. Woods (Leigh)
26 S. Llewellyn (St.Helens)
25 J. Lewthwaite (Barrow)
24 S. McCormick (St.Helens)
24 L. Ward (Keighley)
24 P. Devery (Huddersfield)

GOALS
133 K. Gee (Wigan)
133 H. Palin (Warrington)
115 H.E. Cook (Leeds)
104 A.J. Risman (Workington)
102 G.Langfield (Castleford)
100 J. Ledgard (Leigh)
100 D. Morgan (Swinton)
 93 J. Bawden (Huddersfield)
 90 D. Chalkley (Halifax)
 83 E. Davies (Salford)

(Above) **Wigan's Lions tourists in 1950 are farewelled at Central Park by club captain Cec Mountford as they prepare to board the bus and head for Australia. Left to right: Gordon Ratcliffle, Jack Hilton, Joe Egan, Ken Gee, Cec Mountford, Tommy Bradshaw, Jack Cunliffe and Martin Ryan. Wigan's eighth tourist, Ernie Ashcroft, was going to be picked up *en route* - at Rose Bridge.**

TIMELINE 1951

Whilst the biggest headlines in the world of Rugby League in 1951 were made in faraway Australia and New Zealand by the explosive first French touring team down-under, at home in Britain it was also a year of significant 'firsts.'

On the field nothing surpassed the achievement of Workington Town in being crowd Champions in only their sixth season as members of the Rugby League. Captained, coached and inspired by the legendary Gus Risman, Workington became the first club from outside the game's birth counties of Yorkshire and Lancashire to contest and win a major final. As Risman raised the championship trophy aloft at Manchester's Maine Road on 12th May, 1951, he said it was the greatest achievement of his long career. Workington beat an injury-hit Warrington side to claim the title, after the top-four had finished with the "Wire" in top spot, Wigan second, Workington third and Leigh fourth. Town then ground out an epic "semi-final" win, 8-5, over Wigan at Central Park to dash the 1950 Champions' hopes of retaining their title, although Wigan did have plenty of consolation by winning the Challenge Cup, beating Barrow in the final at Wembley.

(Above)
Wigan's Jack Broome hands off Workington scrum-half Albert Pepperell in the 1951 top-four play-off match at Central Park.

On the international stage, France continued to make headlines even after their team had returned in triumph from Australia. Their first encounter of 1951 back in Europe turned out to be the infamous "Battle of the Boulevard" against the Other Nationalities at Hull, then - three weeks later on 25th November - when they played their first game on home soil since the tour, a rampant French team ran England ragged in Marseille to win by a record margin of 42-13. A crowd of 31,810 noisy and excited paying spectators at the Velodrome stadium was a new record attendance for a game in France, and it was also the very first time they had beaten the English on French soil. The visitors, captained by Ernest Ward, became the first English team to fly to France but their travel plans hit problems when the plane from Manchester airport had a radio malfunction and they could not take off on the Friday as planned. Instead, the players had to stay overnight in Manchester and finally got airborn for Marseille over 24 hours later.

Also in the autumn of 1951, New Zealand were on tour and played a big part in a thrilling Test series with Great Britain - all three Tests were won by the British side, but all by narrow

---

Elsewhere in the world of sport in 1951

*Jackie Milburn scores both goals as Newcaste United beat Blackpool 2-0 in the F.A. Cup Final.
*In the annual unversity boat race on the River Thames, the Oxford boat sinks.
*British boxer Randolph Turpin becomes world middleweight champion when he beats "Sugar" Ray Robinson at Earl's Court. In 131 previous fights Robinson had only lost one before defeat by Turpin.
*The French Rugby Union team got their much sought after first ever victory on English soil when they beat England 11-3 at Twickenham.
*Cricketer Peter May, aged 21, scored a century in his Test debut against South Africa at Headingley.

margins with the Kiwis going very close to victory. It was during this Kiwi tour that Rugby League introduced two very significant new innovations - live television and floodlights. The second Test of the series was broadcast by the BBC live from Swinton's Station Road ground, and the BBC also said they would be keen to televise floodlit games after Bradford Northern announced they were to spend £2,000 to upgrade the speedway lighting at Odsal Stadium to make it suitable for football. When Bradford played their match against the Kiwi tourists under lights on a Wednesday night, 31st October, a remarkable crowd of 29,072 people turned up to see it - the second biggest attendance of the whole tour.

Earlier in the year, in May 1951, the Festival of Britain was celebrated by Rugby League with a special match at Headingley between "Great Britain" and "Australasia," the latter side selected from antipodean players with English clubs. The Australasians won 23-20, and - in an illustration of just how keen the Rugby League were to spread the game - on the very same day, a Welsh X111 played a British Empire X111 at Llanelly.

(Above) **French winger Vincent Cantoni tries to outpace England's Dick Cracknell in the match at Marseille in 1951 which France won 42-13. Cantoni scored two of France's ten tries that day.**

The enthusiasm in South Wales continued as Cardiff entered the Rugby League as a senior club, along with another new professional club at Doncaster, bringing the number of teams in the Northern Rugby League up to 31. A third new name appeared in the fixtures for the 1951-52 season as Liverpool Stanley became Liverpool City, playing at Knotty Ash.

Off the field, there was no shortage of disputes to tax the Rugby League's officials. The Players' Union and Welfare Organisation, led by Chris Brereton, were turned down in their request for a £5 minimum wage during the season; and then, after captaining Wigan to their Challenge Cup victory at Wembley in May, 1951, the New Zealander Cec Mountford announced that he was retiring as a player and, as his contract with Wigan still had a year to run, he returned the relevant amount of money to the club. He was then appointed team manager at Warrington, but Wigan refused to accept his cheque or cancel his contract as a player.

Another burning issue was the growing practice of English clubs signing Rugby Union players from down-under as a result of the transfer-ban preventing them from signing League players. The Australian Rugby League protested very strongly when they found out that Rochdale Hornets had signed three Aussies who were ex-League men who had switched to Union in order to circumnavigate the transfer-ban.

(Above) **Stanford, Cec Kelly and Wally Ellean - three Aussies in the Rochdale colours in 1950 - as Hornets were at the centre of a transfer-ban dispute.**

TOP TEN

1950-51

TRIES
68 B. Bevan (Warrington)
59 L. Cooper (Huddersfield)
42 B. Nordgren (Wigan)
41 E. Gibson (Workington)
40 G. Wilson (Workington)
33 A. Turnbull (Leeds)
33 J. Lawrenson (Workington)
26 S. Llewellyn (St.Helens)
26 A. Naughton (Warrington)
26 G. Tullock (Hull K.R.)

GOALS
155 H.E. Cook (Leeds)
112 J. Perry (Batley)
108 A.J. Risman (Workington)
97 F. Miller (Featherstone)
95 G. Langfield (Castleford)
91 E. Davies (Salford)
86 A. Gregory (Belle Vue R.)
84 J. Gibson (Bramley)
82 H. Palin (Warrington)
70 K. Gee (Wigan)

TIMELINE
1952

The remarkable rise of Workington Town continued in 1952 when they won the Challenge Cup Final at Wembley which, following their Championship success the previous season, meant Gus Risman's team had won both the game's major honours within seven years of becoming a senior club. The quality of open football produced by Workington was illustrated by both their wingers being among the top try-scorers in the game, Johnny Lawrenson with 49 and George "Happy" Wilson with 40. That kind of entertainment continued to draw big crowds to watch Town at Borough Park and their Supporters' Club claimed almost 10,000 members at various locations throughout Cumberland.

Their opponents in the Cup Final were also newcomers to Wembley in Featherstone Rovers who, with former international winger Eric Batten as their player-coach, had enjoyed a famous quarter-final victory over Cup holders and hot favourites Wigan. The 1952 Cup Final was the first to be televised live nationally.

Wigan had the consolation of going on to win the Championship Final, staged at the new venue of Huddersfield Town's Leeds Road ground. With both Joe Egan and Cec Mountford now gone from Central Park, it was Jack Cunliffe who captained Wigan as they beat Bradford Northern, the league leaders, in that Final.

The other major highlight on the pitch was the reclaiming of the Ashes by Great Britain at their first attempt after temporarily losing their grip on them two years earlier in Sydney. The British team of 1952 was captained by Barrow stand-off Willie Horne, and they beat Australia comfortably in the first two Tests to wrap up the series, before the third Test - played at Bradford - degenerated into a brawling affair and was dubbed "The Battle of Odsal."

The Rugby League proposed that the transfer-ban with Australia be extended to cover Rugby Union as well as Rugby League players, and with a ban also in place on players from New Zealand, changes were ahead for the international game. RFL officials opened discussions with their French counterparts in 1952 about the idea of playing Great Britain versus France Test matches to replace the European Championship, due to their fears that the ban would soon mean the end of the Other Nationalities team. They also expressed concern over the future ability to put together a

(Above) Gus Risman has the Challenge Cup after leading Workington Town to victory over Featherstone at Wembley in 1952.

Elsewhere in the world of sport in 1952

*Nat Lofthouse earns the nickname of "The Lion of Vienna" after he scores twice and is knocked out in England's dramatic 3-2 away victory over Austria.
*In the Helsinki Olympic Games, Britain's only gold medal is won by a horse "Foxhunter" - ridden by Colonel Harry Llewellyn in the team show-jumping.
*At those Olympics the Czech Emil Zatopek wins a treble gold in the 5,000m, 10,000m and marathon.
*Newcastle United beat Arsenal 1-0 at Wembley and become the first team to win the F.A. Cup two years in a row this century.
*Rocky Marciano knocks out Jersey Joe Walcott to begin his reign as world heavyweight champion.

(Above) **Featherstone Rovers players are introduced to the Foreign Secretary, Mr. Anthony Eden, at the 1952 Wembley Final.**

(Above) **The Ashes are back home - Great Britain captain Willie Horne receives the Ashes trophy from the Australian team manager before the third Test of the 1952 series at Odsal, with British R.L. officials Gideon Shaw and Bennett Manson looking on.**

Welsh team of the required standard - which was hard to believe when so many top class players from Wales were playing the game and new recruits were still coming north, not least when Leeds paid a record £6,000 fee to tempt Lewis Jones in November 1952. In stark contrast, the League code's hopes of establishing a senior club in Wales were not going well as Cardiff, only half way through their debut season in the Northern Rugby League, 1951-52, found so little public support that the RFL had to provide financial aid to enable them to complete their fixtures and it quickly became apparent they would not continue in the League for a second season.

Television had wasted little time in becoming a subject of controversy as the BBC and the Rugby League held a conference in late 1952 to discuss claims that live television reduced attendances at other games. It was agreed to choose games that caused the least interference, but after further discussions it was decided that the Challenge Cup Final would not be televised again because of its effects on the attendance at the 1952 Final when the crowd for the Workington Town versus Featherstone match was some 22,000 down on the previous Wembley figures.

The International Board met in England in November 1952, with the seaside town of Blackpool the venue. The delegates found themselves locked in a dispute over the play-the-ball rule, which continued to be a source of angst on the field of play. Blackpool itself was making headlines as various stories surfaced about plans to set up a professional Rugby League club in the resort. One report suggested an established Lancashire club was hoping to relocate to Blackpool, but the most likely candidates - Belle Vue Rangers and Liverpool City - both denied it was them.

(Above) **George Langfield, the Castleford scrum-half was a prolific goal-kicker, and was signed by St.Helens during the 1951-52 season.**

TIMELINE 1953

Huddersfield had been Rugby League's glamour team for much of the decade after the War, and they finally managed to parade their talents on the biggest stage when they won the 1953 Challenge Cup Final. As the claret and gold colours were waved in delight at Wembley, Fartown's teenaged stand-off Peter Ramsden had a dream 19th birthday by winning the Lance Todd trophy. Their victory was a popular one throughout the game, not least because their Wembley opponents St.Helens drew

(Above) **Wigan's Chairman Mr. Joe Taylor welcomes Billy Boston to Central Park in 1953 after one of the most important signings ever made by a Rugby League club.**

(Above) **Swinton winger Peter Norburn made his England debut in November 1953, and scored four tries in a 30-22 win over Other Nationalities. And Norburn was playing opposite Lionel Cooper.**

criticism for their rough tactics. Saints were not happy to be the butt of such criticism from some pressmen and booing from the Wembley crowd, and took much pleasure by eeking out quick revenge on Huddersfield by walloping them 46-nil in the top-four play-off at Knowsley Road. St.Helens, under coach Jim Sullivan, had finished as league leaders and went on to beat second placed Halifax to win their first Championship title.

The most bizarre tour Rugby League had seen took place during 1953 when the "American Allstars" visited Australia and New Zealand. Made up of college gridiron footballers, the Americans had never seen Rugby League before they arrived in Austrtalia to be thrown straight in at the deep end. Not surprisingly they were way out of their depth against Australia's best, but that didn't stop the Americans undertaking a second, shorter, tour at the end of 1953 when they visited France in December.

The crowd-pulling appeal of the Cup continued to grow along with Odsal Stadium's potential for housing huge attendances, as a record 69,198 watched the third round tie between Bradford Northern and Huddersfield; and then, a few weeks later, 58,722 were back at Bradford for Huddersfield's semi-final against Wigan, undeterred by a day of gales and torrential rain at the Odsal bowl. This vibrancy and ambition among the top clubs prompted them to splash out big money in their search for new stars - Wigan landed the biggest signing of all when, after a long and dramatic chase, they persuaded the talented young Welshman from Cardiff's Tiger Bay, Billy Boston, to join them.

Elsewhere in the world of sport in 1953

*English football is stunned when they are routed 6-3 by Hungary at Wembley, thus losing at home to a continental side for the first time.

*Stanley Matthews finally got his F.A. Cup winners' medal as he inspires Blackpool to beat Bolton 4-3 in the "Matthews Final" at Wembley. This was the first F.A. Cup Final to be televised in full.

*Jockey Gordon Richards wins the Derby at his 28th attempt - he was also soon to be knighted.

*American golfer Ben Hogan wins the U.S. and British Open titles and also the U.S. Masters title.

*Sheffield Wednesday centre-forward Derek Dooley has to have his leg amputated after he breaks it against Preston North End and gangrene sets in.

Billy made his Central Park debut in the "A" team on 31st October 1953, with 8,525 spectators drawn to see him - and he never lost his star appeal. Even bigger headlines were created when Leigh signed the Olympic sprinter and 100m world record holder Emmanuel McDonald Bailey, in a deal largely negotiated by the journalist Eddie Waring as a spectacular 'scoop' for his newspaper, the *"Sunday Pictorial."* Bailey went on to play just one game of Rugby League, on 16th December 1953, when 14,996 fans rolled up for a specially arranged floodlit "friendly" at Hilton Park against Wigan. McDonald Bailey scored a try, but never played another game.

(Above) **Royal box presentation at Wembley in 1953 as Huddersfield captain Russ Pepperell receives the Cup from the Duke of Norfolk.**

(Above) **Olympic sprinter McDonald Bailey is tackled in a training session at Leigh before his much publicised debut game in Rugby League.**

Meanwhile, an application was received to have Scotland's first professional club join the Rugby League - they were to be the Glasgow Black Eagles and, at an extraordinary general meeting of the Rugby League Council on 30th April 1953, their representative, a Mr. Fraser, said they would play at the White City Stadium in Glasgow which could hold 30,000 spectators with 10,000 under cover, that they already had £5,000 towards the £10,000 guarantee asked by the League, and they would manage on crowds of 5,000. After hearing the Glasgow proposals, the Rugby League's clubs unaminously rejected their application, with travelling difficulties cited as the key factor.

TOP TEN

1952-53

TRIES

72 **B. Bevan** (Warrington)
59 **J. McLean** (Bradford N.)
50 **L. Cooper** (Huddersfield)
47 **B. Nordgren** (Wigan)
46 **P. Henderson** (Huddersfield)
40 **D. Bevan** (Wigan)
39 **S. McCormick** (St.Helens)
37 **D. Greenall** (St.Helens)
35 **S. Llewellyn** (St.Helens)
35 **A. Turnbull** (Leeds)

GOALS

170 **H. Bath** (Warrington)
149 **G. Langfield** (St.Helens)
145 **P. Devery** (Huddersfield)
140 **B. Ganley** (Oldham)
138 **J. Phillips** (Bradford N.)
123 **J. Ledgard** (Leigh)
117 **T. Griffiths** (Doncaster & Halifax)
105 **A. Lunn** (Castleford)
102 **H. Palin** (Halifax & Keighley)
95 **A. Blan** (Swinton)

TIMELINE 1954

(Above)
Dave Valentine, of Huddersfield, became Britain's World Cup hero in 1954

(Right)
The double winning Warrington team are welcomed to the Town Hall by the Mayor with their trophies on show to the crowd. Gerry Helme holds the Lancashire League trophy, skipper Eric Frodsham has the Challenge Cup, and Ally Naughton holds the Championship trophy.

There can be few, if any, more pivotal years in the history of Rugby League than 1954 - a year when the game reached new peaks, both at home and on the international front, which the founding fathers of the Northern Union over a half century earlier could never have envisaged in even their wildest dreams.

1954 was the year when the World Cup was born, and with it one of the most romantic and enduring tales of sporting folklore for the way Scotsman Dave Valentine led his Great Britain team to victory in France in a tournament nobody gave them a chance of winning. Their triumph in a final play-off in Paris was televised live in Britain via the fledgling Eurovision Link, thus providing unprecedented publicity for the Rugby League game as no other British sporting team had ever taken part in a World Cup Final on foreign soil and had their contest beamed back live to the public at home.

Domestically, everything in Rugby League was dwarfed by the incredible crowd which gathered at Odsal Stadium on 5th May 1954 to watch the Challenge Cup Final replay between Halifax and Warrington. The attendance officially given as 102,569 on that Wednesday night in Bradford (although it was generally accepted that the actual figure was many thousands more) was the biggest ever for an English football match outside London. They saw Warrington win the Cup (after they and Halifax had produced a 4-all draw at Wembley) on their first step to a "double." Three days after that famous Odsal replay, the same two teams met in the Championship Final at Maine Road which

Elsewhere in the world of sport in 1954

*The first sub four-minute mile in the history of athletics is run at Oxford's Iffley Road track by Roger Bannister, a 25-year-old medical student.
*Hungary, dubbed the "Magnificent Magyars" are surprisingly beaten 3-2 by Germany in the final of football's World Cup. Earlier in the year Hungary had inflicted a second big defeat on England, 7-1.
*A crowd of 45,000 packed into London's White City to see English athlete Chris Chataway clip five seconds off the world 5,000 metres record.
*Jaroslav Drobny finally wins the Wimbledon tennis championship at his 11th attempt, beating the 19-year-old Australian Ken Rosewall in the final.
*The Union des Associations Europeene de Football (UEFA) is formed.

saw Warrington sneak home by a point, 8-7, despite Halifax scoring the only try by prop-froward John Thorley who, later in the year, was to become one of the World Cup winning heroes. There was no doubt the individual player of 1954 was Gerry Helme, the Warrington scrum-half who was pivotal to his club's "double" and became the first man in history to win the Lance Todd trophy twice, followed by being the master tactician and key try-scorer in Britain's World Cup win.

Helme had also been in the Lions touring team which had run into some huge controversies in Australia and New Zealand, most of which had been "grossly exaggerated" according to the tour manager Mr. Hector Rawson when the British team arrived home with a record £34,000 profit, but no Ashes after being narrowly defeated 2-1 in the third and deciding Test in Sydney. The 1954 Lions were the first to travel by air to Australia.

Rugby League in England was being financially hit by having to pay substantial "entertainment tax" to the exchequer, whilst numerous other sports were not deemed similarly liable. Certainly much ignorance, and possibly some prejudice, was in evidence as Bill Fallowfield attempted to plead Rugby League's case in the corridors of power in London. In 1951-52 the total paid by Rugby League was £46,856, but in 1952-53 this tax payment had risen to £106,241, even though overall attendances had fallen by 12% and receipts by 4%. It was money than many struggling clubs could not afford to lose.

Nevertheless, enthusiasm for the game to spread its wings continued at a pace, and the much anticipated new club at Blackpool finally became reality when, on 6th May 1954, the Rugby League Council voted unanimously to accept the application of Blackpool Borough. A second Italian touring team arrived in England, whilst Australia and New Zealand played each other in Long Beach, California on their way home from the World Cup as hopes continued of developing the game in the United States.

(Above)
An exciting young threequarter emerged at Huddersfield, Mick Sullivan, signed from Shaw Cross Boys Club. By the end of 1954 he would be a World Cup winner.

(Above) **Great Britain defend against New Zealand at a muddy Carlaw Park in Auckland on the 1954 tour. Alf Burnell watches Geoff Gunney, Jim Bowden and Billy Boston get ready to tackle the Kiwis.**

TOP TEN

1953-54

TRIES
67 B. Bevan (Warrington)
52 J. McLean (Bradford N.)
41 A. Turnbull (Leeds)
40 L. Cooper (Huddersfield)
37 S. Llewellyn (St.Helens)
33 K. Bowman (Hull)
32 D. Boocker (Wakefield T.)
32 A. Daniels (Halifax)
32 P. Henderson (Huddersfield)
32 I. Watts (Hull)

GOALS
153 P. Metcalfe (St.Helens)
153 H. Bath (Warrington)
143 J. Phillips (Bradford N.)
140 C. Hutton (Hull)
138 A.J. Risman (Workington.)
124 L. Jones (Leeds)
120 B. Ganley (Oldham)
117 T. Griffiths (Halifax)
116 P. Devery (Huddersfield)
115 J. Ledgard (Leigh)

Barrow achieved their dream of winning the Challenge Cup in 1955 and were the most popular of winners, largely because of the widespread admiration for their captain Willie Horne. No individual can have been a greater talisman figure for, not only a rugby club, but a whole town, as Willie was to Barrow. To get their hands on the Cup, Barrow had to beat Workington Town in an all north-west Final - both clubs enjoying their second visit to Wembley of the decade, although Workington had said goodbye to the charismatic leader of their early days, Gus Risman, with Jim Brough taking over the coaching reins in their run to the 1955 Cup Final.

Another coach making his mark was Warrington's Cec Mountford - after guiding the Wire to a Cup and League "double" in 1954, the New Zealander saw his team retain their Championship in 1955 after beating Oldham in a Maine Road Final somewhat spoiled by bad weather. On an unseasonally muddy pitch in mid May, Warrington were grateful to their prolific try-scorer Brian Bevan for the one which counted in their 7-3 win over Oldham. Cec Mountford was also enlisted to give coaching advice to his fellow countrymen whilst the 1955 Kiwi tour-

(Above)
Jeff Stevenson, the Leeds scrum-half, in action versus the 1955 Kiwis at Headingley. The New Zealanders beat Leeds 18-16.

ing team were in England.

The New Zealanders found themselves the victims of some of unsporting attitudes when, after basing themselves in the pleasant Yorkshire town of Ilkley - which had become the custom for touring teams - they were refused permission to use the local rugby ground for training. Previous Kiwi teams had been made welcome at the ground and the local Ilkley Rugby Union Club said they were willing to continue in this vein, but had been ordered by the Rugby Union to refuse permission. Once in action, the Kiwis were popular visitors but, against very much a new look Great Britain team compared to the one which had won the World Cup only 12 months earlier, they were unable to win the Test series.

The curtain came down on the Other Nationalities team in 1955 as the European International Championship was put into mothballs. Other Nationalities, boosted by the inclusion of Welsh players, went out in style by thrashing both England and France to take the title. The swansong for Wales had come in May 1955, with a 24-11 defeat away to France 'B' in an end of season match played at Nantes. It seemed ironic that the Wales team was being

---

Elsewhere in the world of sport in 1955

*At Le Mans, in France, motor racing's worst ever disaster takes place as cars crash into the crowd, killing 83 people and injuring hundreds more.
*Manchester United's Duncan Edwards becomes the youngest England international of the 20th century at 18 years and 183 days - his debut is v. Scotland.
*In Rugby Union, the British Lions draw their Test series in South Africa 2-2; a young winger named Tom Van Vollenhoven stars for the Springboks.
*British motor-cyclist Geoff Duke wins his third consecutive 500-cc world title.
*Juan Fangio, of Argentina, becomes the world motor racing champion for the third time.

(Pictured) The joy of bringing the Cup back home, as the Barrow team arrive back at Craven Park after an open-top bus parade all the way from Ulverston station on their triumphant return from Wembley in 1955.

disbanded due to a belief that they didn't have enough top quality players, when the Great Britain which played New Zealand the very same year included Welshmen like: Billy Boston, Glyn Moses, Lewis Jones and Arthur Daniels (significantly, all were in the back division.)

The Rugby League's newest club, Blackpool Borough, completed their first season, 1954-55, third from the bottom of the league, but their optimism shone through even stronger when they kicked off the following season's Kiwi tour on 10th September 1955 by drawing a crowd of over 12,000 to see them play the tourists at the local Bloomfield Road football ground. Not only that, the "babes" - as Blackpool were known - achieved a remarkable 24-all draw with the New Zealanders.

In sharp contrast, one of Rugby League's oldest clubs Belle Vue Rangers (who, under their previous moniker of Broughton Rangers had been founder members of the Northern Union in 1895) disappeared at the end of the 1954-55 season after been refused permission to continue using the Belle Vue Gardens stadium, and then being unable to come up with an alternative venue to the satisfaction of the Rugby League Council. The Manchester based club played their final fixture away at Workington's Borough Park on 5th May 1955. This left the Northern Rugby League with 30 member clubs as the 1955-56 season commenced. On the world stage, France enjoyed a second successful tour to Australia in 1955, whilst in England the growth of television continued with the arrival of a second channel, ITV, who sponsored and broadcast a special floodlit competition played at London soccer grounds.

TOP TEN

1954-55

TRIES

66	L. Cooper	(Huddersfield)
63	B. Bevan	(Warrington)
45	P. Henderson	(Huddesfield)
42	A. Turnbull	(Leeds)
34	M. Davies	(Leigh)
33	F. Carlton	(St.Helens)
33	F. Kitchen	(Leigh)
33	T. Lynch	(Halifax)
33	I. Southward	(Workington)
31	B. Boston	(Wigan)
31	A. Davies	(Oldham)

GOALS

178	J. Ledgard	(Leigh)
120	H. Bath	(Warrington)
110	C. Hutton	(Hull)
107	J. Wilson	(Bramley)
104	L. Jones	(Leeds)
95	J. Wood	(Liverpool City)
91	T. Griffiths	(Halifax)
89	D. Fox	(Featherstone R.)
89	B. Ganley	(Oldham)
89	F. Mortimer	(Wakefield T.)

TIMELINE 1956

(Above)
St.Helens captain Alan Prescott is congratulated by Halifax skipper Alvin Ackerley after the 1956 Wembley Final.

S t.Helens won the Challenge Cup in 1956 for the first time in their history, quite a surprise they had to wait so long when one remembers they actually played in the very first Cup Final way back in 1897. It was fitting that the try which sealed their victory at Wembley was scored by their captain, Alan Prescott, a local lad leading his home town team to glory.

Saints beat Halifax at Wembley, and the men from Thrum Hall must have thought they were jinxed in major Finals when they also went on to finish runners-up in the Championship, beaten by a last minute penalty-goal by Hull at Manchester's Maine Road. Halifax, as one of the outstanding teams of the 'fifties, had played in two Challenge Cup Finals (plus a replay) and three Championship Finals between 1953 and 1956 - and lost them all. They must have thought it was finally going to be their year in 1956 after two inspirational semi-final victories, 11-10 over Wigan in the Challenge Cup and then a sweet revenge for Wembley win, 23-8, over St.Helens in the top-four play-off.

But it was Hull who claimed the Championship title, coming from fourth place to inflict a shock 17-nil defeat on Warrington at Wilderspool in the play-off (Warrington having finished as league leaders for the second year in a row), and then upsetting Halifax 10-9 in the Maine Road Final. Hull's win came by courtesy of a late, late penalty kicked by their full-back Colin Hutton from way out on the right-hand touchline. After the game, Hull's captain Mick Scott famously admitted he was about to take a tap when the last minute penalty was awarded so far out and near touch, but he remembered Hutton's words before the match to "give me any kicks inside their half" - so he stuck by his promise to his full-back, and Colin did not let him down.

The magic of the Challenge Cup continued to grow, as 52,273 people turned out at Odsal to see Halifax beat Wigan, and 38,897 at Swinton to watch St.Helens draw 5-5 with Barrow in the other semi-final. The replay, on a Wednesday afternoon at Wigan, attracted a crowd of 44,731 who paid receipts of £7,768 (both new records for Central Park) - there they saw an epic match of almost unbearable tension which finished

---

Elsewhere in the world of sport in 1956

*Rocky Marciano announces his retirement from boxing, the world heavyweight champion had won all 49 professional fights, 43 by knock-out.
*Cricketer Jim Laker takes all 10 wickets in one innings, and 19 wickets in total, in the fourth Ashes test match versus Australia at Old Trafford.
*Football's first European Cup is launched in the 1955-56 season, without the England champions Chelsea. Real Madrid are the first winners.
*Manchester City' goalkeeper, Bert Trautmann plays with a broken neck in the F.A. Cup Final as Don Revie inspires a Wembley win over Birmingham.
*Devon Loch becomes the unluckiest loser of a Grand National as his legs went from under him whilst in the lead just 55 yards from the finish.

(Above)
Jimmy Ledgard, the Leigh full-back and 1954 World Cup star, was the top goal-kicker of 1955-56.

(Above)
Hull's full-back Colin Hutton is unable to stop Arthur Daniels touching down for Halifax in the 1956 Championship Final.

nil-nil after 80 minutes of pulsating cup-tie action. After extra-time, Saints were ahead 10-5 and Wembley bound, thus denying Barrow what would have become three successive Challenge Cup Finals. There was controversy at Wigan after their semi-final loss against Halifax when Billy Boston was suspended indefinitely by the club's Board of Directors.

Great Britain won back the Ashes in 1956 during a Kangaroo tour that was one of the most disappointing on record. Captained by Alan Prescott, the British team had little trouble in winning the deciding Test match 19-nil, and thus set themselves up as strong favourites for the World Cup that was to follow at the end of that season. The 1956 Ashes series was notable in that one of the Tests was staged at Wigan's Central Park for the first time, whilst Headingley missed out after being a regular Test venue since 1911. The Great Britain players were on £14 a win, and £8 a loss, for the Tests against Australia, with several commentators of the day pointing out that this compared unfavourably with England soccer players who got a £50 fee (win or lose) in an international match. Spectators had to pay three shillings for admittance to the Tests at a time when the minimum admission for league and cup games had just been increased from 1s./6d. to two shillings.

During 1956 the Rugby League continued to debate the rules of the game, with particular angst over the play-the-ball. Two trial matches were played at Odsal on 8th October, to experiment with different ways of bringing the ball back into play, but players and fans were left unimpressed. George Phillips, the well known top referee from Widnes, was elected chairman of the referees' committee as the League sought uniformity in the interpretation of the laws. Meanwhile, as an illustration of what was happening in the rest of the world at that time, in December 1956, petrol rationing resulting from the Suez crisis caused the former Halifax forward Harry Beverley to resign from his position as Doncaster's coach. Beverley said he could not travel from his home in Leeds to Doncaster as often as necessary.

TOP TEN

1955-56

TRIES
61 J. McLean (Bradford N.)
57 B. Bevan (Warrington)
49 B. Boston (Wigan)
42 F. Carlton (St.Helens)
41 J. Lewthwaite (Barrow)
40 S. Llewellyn (St.Helens)
38 M. Sullivan (Huddersfield)
34 A. Daniels (Halifax)
29 F. Castle (Barrow)
28 I. Southward (Workington)

GOALS
155 J. Ledgard (Leigh)
154 H. Bath (Warrington)
147 T. Griffiths (Halifax)
138 A. Rhodes (St.Helens)
133 C. Hutton (Hull)
130 J. McKeown (Whitehaven)
122 J. Phillips (Bradford N.)
113 W. Horne (Barrow)
110 F. Dyson (Huddersfield)
102 J. Fennell (Featherstone R.)

Oldham were widely respected as the game's best footballing team in the mid-'fifties and they finally got their reward in 1957 by being crowned Champions. The "Roughyeds" finished top of the table at the end of the 1956-57 season, losing only five of their 38 matches, and six points ahead of second-placed Hull. It was the "Airlie Birds" who provided opposition in the Championship Final which, just as in the previous year, went right down to the wire with the Hull full-back, Colin Hutton, having a late goal-kick to win the match - but, this time, Colin missed and Oldham prevailed 15-14 to win the Championship they surely deserved.

It was a great season for Oldham as they won three of the famous "all four" cups, taking both the Lancashire League and Cup - but the Wembley trip they craved continued to prove elusive as they were knocked out of the Challenge Cup 5-nil away at Leigh in terrible conditions. But, despite all the success at Watersheddings, in April 1957 the Oldham committee were faced with a potential mutiny by their players who sent a letter, signed by ten of those players, asking that the coach Griff Jenkins not be re-engaged when his contract expired.

Leeds won the Challenge Cup in 1957, their first Wembley triumph since 1936, just nosing two points ahead of Barrow (back at Wembley for the third time in six years). Again the battle to get to Wembley produced herculean struggles in the semi-finals, with Whitehaven losing to Leeds 10-9 thanks to a late, and controversial, Jeff Stevenson drop-goal, whilst Barrow and Leigh were fighting out a 2-all draw - Willie Horne's men taking the replay 15-10.

International matches between Great Britain and France were finally given full Test status in 1957, and the second World Cup tournament was staged in Australia in which the British team - hot favourites to win - succumbed to the host nation and relinquished the title won so gloriously by Dave Valentine's team in France three years earlier. On the way home from the 1957 World Cup, the British and French teams were invited to South Africa where they played each other in three exhibition games in. As a promotional vehicle for Rugby League, the games were a flop, as the French team were not competitive, leaving spectators far from impressed. But at the same time a far more positive link with South Africa was being developed by Rugby League clubs - with the transfer ban with Australia renewed for a further three years, they started to look to South

(Above)
Tom van Vollenhoven in his debut match for St.Helens against Leeds at Knowsley Road in October 1957.

Elsewhere in the world of sport in 1957

*Stanley Matthews plays his last game for England aged 42, although he will not retire from League football until 1965.

*The Football League again try to persuade their champions not to enter the European Cup. However, unlike Chelsea in 1955-56, Manchester United refuse to bow to such pressure as manager Matt Busby is eager to "meet the European challenge."

*Australian Lew Hoad becomes only the third man in history to retain the Wimbledon tennis singles championship for a second year in a row.

African Rugby Union as a new source of imports to excite their fans. The earliest signings included Ronnie Colin to Hunslet, and Tom van Vollenhoven to St.Helens - the latter going on to be one of the greatest stars the game has known. Vollenhoven signed for Saints for £4,000 and made his debut at Knowsley Road against Leeds on 25th October 1957. Tom scored a try, and the rest became history.

Three of the most popular and successful Australians to grace British Rugby League were ready to hang up their boots in 1957, all after a decade at the top. Harry Bath (Warrington) and Johnny Hunter (Huddersfield) headed home to Australia at the end of the '56-'57 season, whilst Arthur Clues (Hunslet) called it a day on the rugby field but stayed in Leeds where he owned a very successful sports outfitters business in the city.

(Above) European Club Champions - Hull line up alongside the Carcassonne team in France before their match in the competition played in 1956-57 between England's top two clubs of the previous seasons, Hull and Halifax, and their French counterparts Carcassonne and Albi. The "Airlie Birds" were unbeaten and won the Euro' title.

TOP TEN

1956-57

TRIES

60 **B. Boston** (Wigan)
51 **J. Lewthwaite** (Barrow)
48 **J. Freeman** (Halifax)
43 **J. Etty** (Oldham)
37 **W. Kindon** (Leigh)
36 **L. Jones** (Leeds)
34 **A. Snowden** (Hunslet)
33 **F. Carlton** (St.Helens)
33 **S. Llewellyn** (St.Helens)
33 **M. Sullivan** (Huddersfield)

GOALS

194 **L. Jones** (Leeds)
189 **B. Ganley** (Oldham)
166 **C. Hutton** (Hull)
149 **J. McKeown** (Whitehaven)
148 **F. Dyson** (Huddersfield)
145 **A. Rhodes** (St.Helens)
135 **J. Ball** (Barrow)
123 **G. Langfield** (Bramley)
118 **V. Yorke** (York)
117 **F. Mortimer** (Wakefield T.)

TIMELINE 1958

In a year that will always be remembered in Rugby League for its sensational Lions tour on which Great Britain retained the Ashes in Australia in the most heroic style, domestically many of the headlines were made by Workington Town. The Cumbrian club's impact on the 1958 Lions touring team was significant, with four players involved plus a manager and the coach who were at the centre of the dramas and controversies which led to a Rugby League Council inquest; and at home Town qualified for both the Challenge Cup and Championship Finals. They achieved this following a tremendous run of success in the second half of the 1957-58 season - after losing at Bramley on 14th December they won 18 successive league games and four Cup ties. Their one and only defeat before the Wembley Final was at Oldham on 26th April, their last league fixture.

Workington's luck ran out in those two major Finals with injuries wrecking their hopes in both. At Wembley, with Brian Edgar, Harry Archer and Andy Key all sustaining injuries, Wigan beat Town 13-8 to win the Cup in their first Final under the captaincy of Eric Ashton. Seven days later in the Championship Final against Hull at Odsal, Workington again found themselves playing a man short after Cec Thompson was carried off and Johnny Whiteley's men took the title convincingly. It was Hull's third successive Championship Final, and they won it from fourth place after finishing 11 points behind Oldham, league leaders for the second year running. It was a big disappointment for both the top two clubs, Oldham and St.Helens, who lost at home to Hull and Workington respectively in the top-four play-offs - Oldham, the reigning Champions, being particulary unfortunate as they had lost only four of their 38 league matches.

Once again, Oldham's Wembley dream had been shattered when their confidence of treading the famous turf had been stronger than ever. They were beaten by Wigan in the quarter-final, at Watersheddings - a result which ended a sequence of 14 consecutive Oldham wins over Wigan. It was a shattering defeat for the "Roughyeds," their fans' disappointment made worse when it turned out their semi-final opponents would have been neighbours Rochdale. The Hornets, with Italian Ferdi "Corsi" on the wing, gave Wigan an almighty battle in the semi-final, losing by only 5-3, and going as close

(Above)
Ike Southward, the Workington winger, reaches for a pass in the 1958 Wembley Final, as stand-off Harry Archer is sent reeling by a challenge from Mick Sullivan of Wigan.

Elsewhere in the world of sport in 1958

*The plane carrying the Manchester United team crashes in snow at Munich airport on 6th February, leaving seven players and three club officials among 21 people who lost their lives.
*Brazil win the soccer World Cup, staged in Sweden, and introduce a new 17-year-old star called Pele.
*In golf, Arnold Palmer wins his first U.S. Masters title, at the age of 28. He will win another three.
*In Rugby Union, France makes its first southern hemisphere tour, winning narrowly in South Africa.

(*Above*) Despair for Oldham ... joy for Wigan, as Brian McTigue scores a crucial try in the 1958 Cup quarter-final at Watersheddings. Bernard Ganley holds McTigue but cannot prevent the touchdown. Wembley-bound Wigan won 8-nil.

(*Above*) Joe Phillips the Keighley full-back who kicked 106 goals in the 1957-58 season. Joe was one of the five New Zealanders signed by Bradford Northern in 1950 - he gave fine service at Odsal before moving to Lawkholme Lane.

as they ever managed to Wembley. At least Oldham did ensure they entered the record books when their full-back, Bernard Ganley, finished the 1957-58 season with a total of 219 goals, and thus became the first man ever in senior Rugby League to kick more than 200 goals in a season.

One man who did not have the best of luck in 1958 was Halifax winger Johnny Freeman. After scoring 48 tries and setting a new Halifax club record in 1956-57, the Welsh flyer Freeman began the following campaign in devastating form and even before Christmas had scored 38 tries in just 20 matches.

That kind of scoring ratio meant Johnny was on course to rival Rugby League's all time tries-in-a-season record of 80, by Albert Rosenfeld, which had stood since 1914. Alas, on 21st December 1957, Johnny Freeman badly injured his knee playing for Halifax at Batley and was out of the game for almost a year - not only was the chance gone of breaking that previously "untouchable" record, so was an almost certain place in the 1958 Lions touring team.

Boothferry Park in Hull had already staged several Rugby League games, and the practice of utilising the floodlights at big soccer grounds expanded in the autumn of 1958 when, first, Hunslet played Leeds at Elland Road (and described the crowd of 19,289 as disappointing) and then Salford entertained Leeds at Manchester's Old Trafford.

(*Above*) Johnny Freeman of Halifax - injury stopped him making big headlines in 1958.

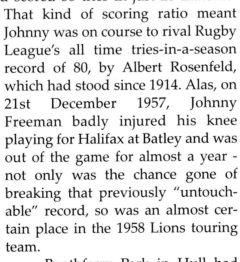

TOP TEN

1957-58

TRIES

50	M. Sullivan	(Hudds. & Wigan)
47	I. Southward	(Workington T.)
46	B. Bevan	(Warrington)
45	M. Davies	(Bradford N.)
43	B. Boston	(Wigan)
41	E. Ashton	(Wigan)
40	T. Van Vollenhoven	(St.Helens)
40	K. Williams	(Halifax)
38	J. Freeman	(Halifax)
32	B. Smith	(York)
32	F. Castle	(Barrow)
32	N. Fox	(Wakefield T.)
32	I. Watts	(Hull)

GOALS

219	B. Ganley	(Oldham)
148	V. Yorke	(York)
139	L. Jones	(Leeds)
138	P. Bateson	(Hull)
124	N. Fox	(Wakefield T.)
118	H. Dawson	(Widnes)
116	J. Cunliffe	(Wigan)
113	P. Walshaw	(Batley)
106	J. Phillips	(Keighley)
103	J. Ball	(Barrow)

TIMELINE
1959

As the decade of the 'Fifties headed towards its close, Rugby League found itself with the two Lancashire giants, Wigan and St.Helens, at the top of the tree, and the Ashes safely retained by Great Britain on home soil as usual - with nobody in their right mind being able to predict it would be the last time we would be able to say that.

St.Helens were at their swashbuckling best as they stormed to the Championship title in 1959, with their stars returned from the 1958 Lions tour stepping up several gears with their confidence so high - notably Alex Murphy, Vinty Karalius, Abe Terry, Dick Huddart (signed from Whitehaven shortly after the tour) and skipper Alan Prescott recovered from his broken arm. In addition, Saints had their new sensation Tom van Vollenhoven in his first full season in the game, finishing as the League's top try-scorer and setting a new St.Helens club record. They had a

(Above)
Vinty Karalius - who came back from the 1958 Austraian tour with the nickname "The Wild Bull of the Pampas" - proved to be a towering figure in St.Helens winning the Championship title in 1959.

second South African flyer on the other wing in Jan Prinsloo, and Saints became the first team in Rugby League history to score more than 1,000 points in a season. They finished top of the league and easily disposed of Oldham, 42-4, in the top-four play-off, to set up a Championship Final against Hunslet. The men from Parkside, captained by Brian Shaw, had shocked most tipsters by beating Wigan at Central Park in their own Championship semi-final, and proceeded to give St.Helens a real run for their money in an Odsal Final which turned out to be an orgy of points scoring. The heatwave conditions played a part in an unprecedented scoreline of 44-22,

(Above) **Mick Martyn of Leigh, played for Great Britain in 1959.**

but there was no denying the brilliance of Saints' attacking play, especially from Murphy and a memorable hat-trick by Vollenhoven.

The Challenge Cup Final of 1959 was also a high scoring affair, but much more one sided, as Wigan easily beat Hull 30-13 and Eric Ashton became the first captain to lift the Cup at Wembley in two consecutive years. By this time, Wigan also had a star from southern Africa in their full-back Fred "Punchy" Griffiths, and he kicked six goals in his first appearance at Wembley.

Whilst debate continued in 1959 on Rugby League's fixture formula, amid constant cries for a switch to two divisions and threats of a "super" league breakaway when the required two-thirds majority vote remained elusive in the Rugby League Council chamber, the crowd-pulling power of the big games (especially Cup ties) was undeniable, and on Good Friday, 1959

Wigan set a new attendance record for a regular league fixture when 47,747 packed into Central Park for their match with St.Helens. The vibrancy of the sport meant clubs were paying big transfer-fees in their seach for success, and in March 1959 the first five figure fee was achieved when a new record of £10,500 was paid by Oldham to Workington Town for their international winger Ike Southward. That came shortly after Oldham had received £8,000 - a record fee for a forward - from Wakefield Trinity for Derek Turner, and later in the year Oldham themselves broke that record when they paid Whitehaven £9,000 for their loose-forward Geoff Robinson.

Television coverage of the game was growing, and so was the controversy among clubs who complained that live broadcasts hit their attendances, but the die was cast when the Rugby League Management Committee announced in the summer of 1959 that they had signed a contract with the BBC to televise a minimum of 13 League games in the forthcoming season. That television coverage became an even bigger issue during the Kangaroo tour in the autumn of 1959, as the Aussies returned for their third visit of the decade, only to go home empty handed yet again.

(Above)
Mick Sullivan just beat Leigh's Brian Fallon to score the only try of the Cup semi-final at Swinton which sent Wigan to Wembley in 1959 for the second year in a row. Brave Leigh lost narrowly ... 5-nil.

(Above) **Geoff Gunney dives over to score for Hunslet against Huddersfield at Parkside. Hunslet won through to the 1959 Championship Final and played their part in a spectacular.**

TOP TEN

1958-59

TRIES
62 T. Van Vollenhoven (St.Helens)
54 B. Bevan (Warrington)
54 B. Boston (Wigan)
40 G. Hemingway (Leeds)
38 I. Southward (Work'tn. & Oldham)
37 A. Murphy (St.Helens)
37 F. Smith (Wakefield T.)
34 F. Myler (Widnes)
34 M. Sullivan (Wigan)
33 W. Walker (Hunslet)

GOALS:
190 B. Ganley (Oldham)
181 W. Langton (Hunslet)
176 F. Griffiths (Wigan)
165 P. Fearis (St.Helens)
148 N. Fox (Wakefield T.)
128 C. Kellett (Hull K.R.)
127 V. Yorke (York)
126 L. Jones (Leeds)
121 E. Fraser (Warrington)
120 S. Thompson (Batley)

That incredible night at Odsal

THE RUGBY LEAGUE CHALLENGE CUP COMPETITION
FINAL TIE
HALIFAX v. WARRINGTON

ODSAL STADIUM, BRADFORD
WEDNESDAY, 5th MAY, 1954

Official Programme — Sixpence

(Above)
Programme for the Odsal Cup Final replay of 1954.

In the history of British sport, nothing could match the incredible scenes at Bradford's Odsal Stadium on the evening of May 5th, 1954, as a crowd of 102,569 was recorded for the replay of the Challenge Cup Final between Halifax and Warrington. Estimates put the actual attendance figure at in excess of 120,000 - nobody will ever know the truth - but it was an iconic moment in the story of Rugby League. Typically, such fantastic scenes which would have rocked the nation had they occurred in any other sport, went largely unreported outside the north of England. It raised the question in many circles about bringing the Challenge Cup Final "back home" to the north, and away from Wembley. Some correspondents claimed it was a sign that Rugby League followers flocked to Odsal to make a statement of protest against "expensive London prices" and the cost of travelling to the capital for the game's showpiece.

Whatever truth there may, or may not, have been in such thinking, it was indisputable that everyone had been taken by surprise by the sheer size of the crowd that night in Bradford. In the lead up to the replay, the Rugby League's Cup Committee agreed to put back the kick-off time from 6.30 pm to 7.00 pm, to help surmount rush hour traffic difficulties in Bradford, but nobody was expecting so many people. The *"Yorkshire Post"* newspaper wrote: "If the ground record of 70,198 is approached, which seems

(Left)
Action from the 1954
Wembley Final, as
Warrington's prop
Dan Naughton and
winger Stan
McCormick get down
to a loose-ball, with
the Halifax forwards
Albert Fearnley and
Jack Wilkinson
closing in. The teams
drew 4-4 to create the
need for that replay at
Odsal Stadium.

doubtful in view of travelling difficulties ..." Spectators poured into Odsal from 5.00 pm onwards, and even by half-time of the match some were still trying to get into the ground. The roads were jammed for miles around with the streets of Oldham, on the other side of the Pennines, gridlocked as a convoy of vehicles carrying Warrington supporters attempted to reach Bradford. Many didn't make it in the traffic chaos and had to content themselves with listening to the BBC broadcast on the radio of their coaches.

The replay came about because the two teams drew 4-all in the Final at Wembley on 25th April in a match attended by 81,841. With no mention of any replay arrangements in the Wembley programme, and just a week and half to make ready for the follow-up at Odsal, the omens were that all might not run smoothly. Those of the 100,000 plus inside the stadium who were able to see much of the pitch on 5th May 1954, saw Warrington emerge triumphant by 8 points to 4 to claim victory over Halifax and take the Cup back to Wilderspool. The Yorkshire side were unlucky, with claims for tries disallowed by the referee Mr. Ron Gelder, but they battled toe-to-toe with Warrington in what turned out to be a thrilling Cup-tie, and the antedote to the original meeting at Wembley which was described as a dull affair. It took a brilliant individual try by scrum-half Gerry Helme to win the game for Warrington. Helme beat man after man on a mesmersing run to touch down near the corner-flag in the second-half.

The official attendance of 102,569 was the biggest ever in England for a midweek football game and the biggest ever outside of London. On Odsal terracing made up of wooden sleepers and cinder banks, it was a miracle that nobody was hurt, with those who had fainted the only reported casualties. The seating capacity at Odsal that night was 8,000 - made up of 1,000 Old Stand tickets at 25 shillings, 4,500 New Stand tickets at 10/6 and 3,000 ringside tickets at six shillings, with standing room for a reported 100,000 at three shillings each. In the event, the receipts totalled £18,623 - compared to the £29,706 taken at Wembley from a crowd over 20,000 smaller. Three days on from that emotion-sapping night at Odsal, the same two teams met again in the Championship Final at Maine Road, Warrington sealing a double by winning 8-7. One of the reasons blamed for a surprisingly small crowd of 36,519 turning up for that game was people's fears of another crush like Odsal.

(Above)
The captains, Eric
Fordsham and Alvin
Ackerley, lead the two
teams out through the
crowd for the Odsal
replay in 1954.

Even after two Cup
Finals and then the
Championship Final
against each other, the
season wasn't over for
Warrington and
Halifax. The two
teams travelled to
Ireland where they
played each other in
two exhibition games
- the first at Windsor
Park, Belfast in front
of 10,000 people, and
24 hours later at
Dalymount Park in
Dublin where a crowd
of 15,000 was thrilled
by the attacking rugby
produced.

Laying down the laws

(Above)
One of the greats - Tom van Vollenhoven welcomed to St.Helens in 1957 by legendary coach Jim Sullivan.

Apart from arguing over whether to allow live television of games, the subject which caused most sleepless nights for Rugby League Council members throughout the 'Fifties was the play-the-ball rule. Most people were happy with most things about the game on the field, except for the rather crucial matter of how to bring the ball back into play following a tackle. At various times, in various parts of the world, defending teams had to get back one yard, three yards, occasionally five yards, and sometimes no yards at all. The brilliant French touring team of 1951 were delighted to find the Australians experimenting with a five-yard rule that year, as it opened up the game perfectly for their free-slowing style. But when France returned to Australia in 1955, they had to play under a one-yard rule, which the French thought restricted them to a more forward-dominated game.

Although the Chairman of the Rugby League Council was, in theory, the most powerful man in the British game, there's no doubt that the driving force behind anything to do with the laws of the game was League secretary Bill Fallowfield. His particular obsession was with possession being retained at the play-the-ball, and at regular intervals he pushed through various trials involving experimental rules, one of which aped the Rugby Union method of releasing the ball after a tackle. It was not a popular move, and the quality of football produced by the game's great teams and so many wonderfully skilful players during the 1950s - backed up by the huge crowds and public interest generated by big games, especially Cup ties - supported many people's belief that there was absolutely nothing wrong with rules of Rugby League so long as the teams played with the right attitude.

(Above)
Oldham's brilliant Championship team, captained by Bernard Ganley and coached by Griff Jenkins.

That didn't always happen, of course, and there were criticisms of teams hogging possession and playing safety-first tactics. A particularly notorious example of this came in the 1957 Challenge Cup semi-final at Odsal Stadium between Whitehaven and Leeds as the Cumbrian side tried to hold on to a one-point lead in the final stages of the match. One man's nailbiting drama was another man's "creeping barrage" and at the start of the 1958-59 season, the Rugby League introduced a new rule to try and force the acting half-back to pass the ball, by saying that a scrum would be formed if he was caught in possession. It was several years later, in 1966, that Bill Fallowfield finally got his way and the four-tackle rule was introduced, thus changing the game forever - but anybody who saw and admired the brilliant and artistic footballers of the 'Fifites must still wonder why it had to come to that. It is inconceivable to think that the many thousands of people who watched some of the great club sides like: Huddersfield, Gus Risman's Workington, Jim Sullivan's St.Helens, Warrington, Willie Horne's Barrow, Hull, Halifax or Oldham, ever thought there was much wrong with Rugby League as they knew it.

R. L. Council Chairmen

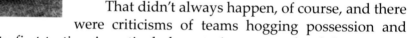

1949-50 - H. HORNBY *(Bradford N.)*
1950-51 - A. WIDDESON *(Lancs. Amateurs)*
1951-52 - Sir EDWIN AIREY *(Leeds)*
1952-53 - B. MANSON *(Swinton)*
1953-54 - C.W. ROBINSON *(York)*
1954-55 - J. HILTON *(Leigh)*
1955-56 - G. OLDROYD *(Dewsbury)*
1956-57 - H. RAWSON *(Hunslet)*
1957-58 - C.E. HORSFALL *(Halifax)*
1958-59 - F. RIDGWAY *(Oldham)*
1959-60 - W. CUNNINGHAM *(Huddersfield)*

Fans could read all about it

New clubs join the League

(Above) **The Doncaster team which played before their record 10,000 crowd in February 1952. Left to right:** *(Standing):* **Jones, Doyle, Norbury, Gronow, Carty, Street, Williams.** *(In front):* **Tynan, Griffiths, Davies, Clough, Price and Heritage.**

(Above)
The Dons hefty pack give no respite to their opponents in this match from their opening season at the York Road Stadium.

After the successful addition of two clubs from Cumberland - at Workington and Whitehaven - in the late 1940s, the Rugby League was eager to expand further at senior level as they entered the 'fifties. The two towns which had long been targeted as potential venues for new professional clubs were Doncaster in South Yorkshire, and Blackpool on the Lancashire coast. Doncaster was a mining area, with long established amateur teams, and Blackpool was the entertainment capital of the north of England, eager to put on new attractions for its thousands of holiday-makers.

Doncaster were the first to make it to the starting line when they entered the Northern Rugby League in the 1951-52 season - playing alongside fellow newcomers Cardiff and the renamed Liverpool City. The new Doncaster club obtained use of the York Road Greyhound Stadium, whose groundsman in 1951 was Isaiah Piper - one of the original shareholders in the new venture and the father of Stuart Piper, who was to become one of Doncaster's loyalest and longest serving players in later years.

A share capital of £8,000 was raised and the "Dons" adopted the colours of royal blue jerseys with a broad gold band and white shorts. From a list of eleven applicants they appointed Gareth Price as their player-manager. A former Leeds and Welsh international centre, Price was signed from Halifax for a fee of £1,000 and he put together a team ready to play Doncaster's first match on 18th August 1951, at home to Wakefield Trinity. An official attendance of 7,600 were there to see the "Dons" get off to a winning start 10-3, although when the turnstiles could not cope with the mass of spectators trying to get in, a fence

Cardiff's single season

(Above) **Cardiff on the defensive against Wigan at Central Park in 1951 - the Welsh side lost 72-5.**

Cardiff emerged from the Welsh League to become a senior club as members of the Northern Rugby League in the 1951-52 season, but their move proved to be ill advised. Way out of their depth on the field, Cardiff took some huge hammerings and conceded over 1,000 points during the season. They could not attract the crowds needed to survive to their Penarth Road stadium, and the Rugby League had to finance them to ensure their fixtures were completed. Cardiff's demise came after one season.

(Left)
Blackpool Borough
are up and running at
the St.Anne's Road
Stadium as centre
David Peace (a
Yorkshireman) takes a
kick in their opening
home game in 1954.
The Borough lost to
Batley 10-7 and had to
wait until 27th
November before they
got their first win,
19-3 at home to Hull
Kingston Rovers.

was broken and it was estimated that over 1,000 people got free access - making the actual attendance anything between 9,000 and 10,000. That five figure crowd was achieved officially later in their first season when Doncaster entertained Bradford in the Challenge Cup at the York Road Stadium. The "Dons" first season was highly successful as they achieved 11th place in the League (of 31 clubs.)

(Above)
The Blackpool team during their debut season, 1954-55, before playing Wigan at Central Park for the first time in October 1954. They are: left to right: (Standing): Fisher, Armitt, Rika, Peace, Duffy, Fishwick, Wright. (In front): Reece, Fleming, Ryder, Emmitt, Wilkinson and Bebe.

Blackpool finished their first season in 29th place in a league of 31 clubs, with only Belle Vue Rangers and Dewsbury below them.

Meanwhile, in west Lancashire, moves to create a professional Rugby League club in Blackpool had been on-going since 1950, with various stadium schemes mooted, before definite plans took shape in late 1953. A Supporters' Club was formed after a meeting in the Majestic Ballroom, and by February 1954 Blackpool Borough Rugby League Club Limited had been launched with a targeted capital of £15,000 in shares of £1 each. The honorary secretary-manager of the new club was Chris Brockbank, the former Warrington secretary who had moved to live and run a business in Blackpool. Mr. Brockbank did an excellent job in recruiting players for the new team, his most important signing being Ron Ryder, the Warrington and Great Britain centre, who became Blackpool's inaugral player-coach. Like Doncaster, the Blackpool club began life playing at a greyhound stadium, the St.Anne's Road Stadium, and they adopted the attractive colours of tangerine, black and white (tangerine being the Blackpool town colours made famous by their football club.)

Borough quickly became known as the "babes" throughout the Rugby League, but they did not have much luck from the fixture planners as they began life with an away match, at Salford on 14th August 1954, and were soundly thrashed 40-3, before making their home debut midweek against Batley. It was hardly the high profile launch the Blackpool directors had hoped for as only 3,000 watched the Batley game. A sign of their real potential came when their first Saturday home fixture against St.Helens drew over 8,000. Just over 12 months later, at the start of their second season, Blackpool drew a crowd of 12,000 at the Bloomfield Road football ground as they achieved a 24-all draw against the New Zealander touring team.

The big media personalities

Throughout the 1950s, Rugby League enjoyed the benefits of having a trio of big personalities, who never failed to promote the game in the media at any opportunity. Harry Sunderland and Eddie Waring had both travelled the same road from team manager, to newspaper reporter, to broadcaster. The chirpy Australian, Sunderland, was winding down his media career as the 'fities drew to a close - whilst Waring, the Dewsbury lad, was seeing his career take off as part of the new age of television in his role as the BBC's voice of Rugby League. Eddie was already the top news reporter with the *"Sunday Pictorial"* and he added a lively new dimension to the game's literature when he brought out his first Annual in 1959. Meanwhile, the third of this trio of big personalities, Jim Windsor - the Leeds based club owner and pools promoter - was a great sponsor and benefactor of publications which celebrated landmarks in the game, calling on his old pal Harry Sunderland to author them.

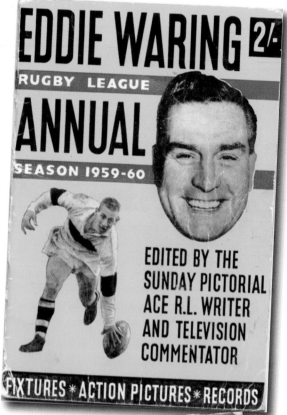

EDDIE WARING 2/-

RUGBY LEAGUE

ANNUAL

SEASON 1959-60

EDITED BY THE SUNDAY PICTORIAL ACE R.L. WRITER AND TELEVISION COMMENTATOR

FIXTURES * ACTION PICTURES * RECORDS

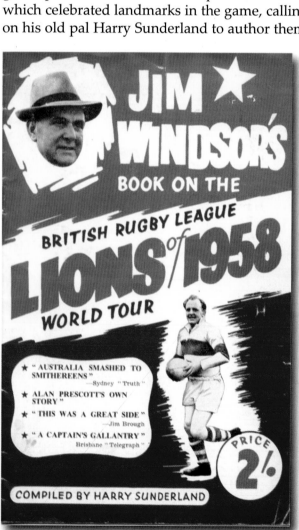

JIM WINDSOR'S BOOK ON THE BRITISH RUGBY LEAGUE LIONS of 1958 WORLD TOUR

★ "AUSTRALIA SMASHED TO SMITHEREENS"
—Sydney "Truth"
★ ALAN PRESCOTT'S OWN STORY"
★ "THIS WAS A GREAT SIDE"
—Jim Brough
★ "A CAPTAIN'S GALLANTRY"
Brisbane "Telegraph"

PRICE 2/-

COMPILED BY HARRY SUNDERLAND

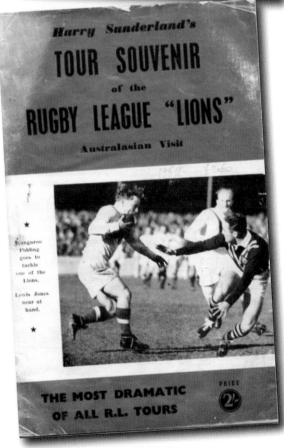

Harry Sunderland's

TOUR SOUVENIR

of the

RUGBY LEAGUE "LIONS"

Australasian Visit

Kangaroo Pidding goes to tackle one of the Lions.

Lewis Jones near at hand.

THE MOST DRAMATIC OF ALL R.L. TOURS

PRICE 2/-

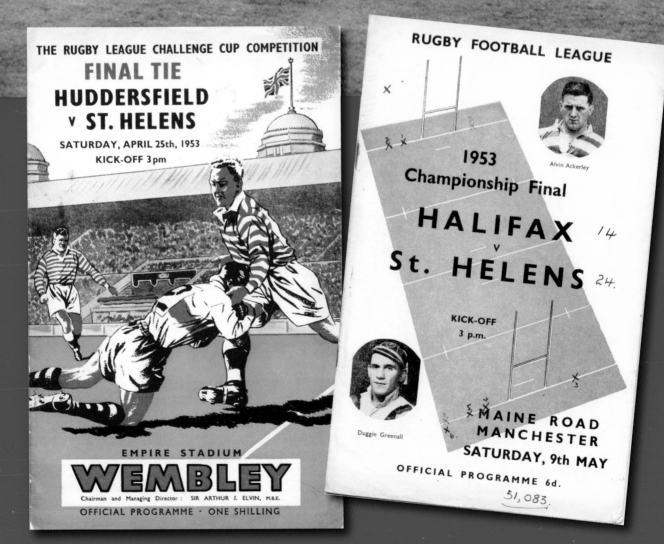

Images of Coronation year

1953

THE RUGBY LEAGUE CHALLENGE CUP COMPETITION
FINAL TIE
HUDDERSFIELD v ST. HELENS
SATURDAY, APRIL 25th, 1953
KICK-OFF 3 pm

EMPIRE STADIUM
WEMBLEY
Chairman and Managing Director : SIR ARTHUR J. ELVIN, M.B.E.
OFFICIAL PROGRAMME · ONE SHILLING

RUGBY FOOTBALL LEAGUE
Alvin Ackerley

1953
Championship Final
HALIFAX v St. HELENS
14
24.
KICK-OFF
3 p.m.
Duggie Greenall
MAINE ROAD
MANCHESTER
SATURDAY, 9th MAY
OFFICIAL PROGRAMME 6d.
51,083.

R.L.'s Television take off

By far the biggest innovation of the 1950s was the arrival of television - and from the very minute television coverage of Rugby League was launched it became a source of argument and controversy. The first match to be televised live nationally from the north of England was on 10th November 1951; the Great Britain versus New Zealand second Test at Swinton. The BBC said they were delighted with the thrilling spectacle at Station Road and were keen to televise another game - but, right away, there were concerns from the clubs about a drop in their own attendances that Saturday afternoon. This was the juggling act the Rugby League had to deal with for the rest of the decade: the value of the national publicity provided by live television versus the effect on actual attendances in the stadiums.

Almost immediately after that Swinton Test match in November 1951, the BBC announced that they would like to televise a league game, Leeds v. Warrington due to be played on 12th January 1952 - but Leeds refused, so Wigan offered their home game versus Wakefield Trinity. And the unrest over television coverage spread rapidly to Australia, where their League officials were anxious that gates for their forthcoming Kangaroo tour in 1952 should not be hit by live t.v. broadcasts. Panic among the Aussies was fuelled by the comments of Mr. Harry "Jersey" Flegg, the 73-year-old chairman of the Australian Board of Control who issued a statement saying: *"The Board will not permit the BBC to use players' services without a very high payment ... the propaganda angle of television does not interest Australia."*

Such comments quickly put the Australians at odds with English League secretary Bill Fallowfield, who was a visionary who recognised the huge potential of television and the need for Rugby League to take advantage of it rather than "close their eyes and pretend it's going to go away."

(Above)
Young Keighley fans and members of the 1952 Australian touring team are fascinated by the live pictures of television, as Eddie Waring hosted a broadcast from Lawkholme Lane on the eve of the Kangaroos' opening tour match.

Throughout the 1950s, Fallowfield faced a battle in trying to convince Rugby League club officials of the wider benefits of embracing television coverage. The 1952 Challenge Cup Final at Wembley was the first to be televised live across the nation by the BBC, and there were complaints that the attendance of 72,093 was well down on the 90,000-plus figures attracted in the several preceding years - although, both the 1952 finalists, Workington and Featherstone, were from smaller towns unable to generate to the size of support of many others. Despite that, the t.v. "doubters" got their way and there were no more Wembley Final broadcasts until 1958. Over-riding the views of "Jersey" Flegg, the 1952 Australian tourists quickly found themselves discovering television when their opening fixture at Keighley was broadcast live as the BBC's desire for more Rugby League gathered pace. After the England versus France international at Odsal in November 1953 was televised, many clubs protested that the broadcast had affected their gates, but the Rugby League Council decided almost unanimously to allow as many matches as possible to be televised - so the future die appeared to be cast, club protests or not. The League's management committee accepted a BBC offer of £150 to televise the 1954 Championship Final, but turned down an offer of £350 for the Challenge Cup Final - the BBC increased their offer to £500 but, when they asked for a reply by 8th April, and the next Rugby League meeting was on the 9th April, the BBC withdrew their offer. Such was the haphazard nature of television contract negotiations in those early days.

The biggest publicity boost the Rugby League game had ever enjoyed came when the first World Cup Final in November 1954 was televised live from Paris via the new Eurovision Link. But, instead of enjoying this gloriously prestigious moment and looking to build upon it, the game found many of its clubs and commentators up in arms at the way domestic club matches that memorable day had experienced a major drop in attendances. The following month, in December 1954, the league's management committee recommended that the BBC should not advertise in advance which league fixtures they were going to televise, and in February 1955 the Yorkshire Federation of Supporters' Club put forward a motion suggesting the banning of the live televising of games. So, Bill Fallowfield was still being faced with a tough battle to persuade club officials and supporters of the overall benefits of the small screen.

In April 1955 the BBC offered £350 to television the Challenge Cup Final, or a contract of £450 for three years. The Rugby League turned it down so the BBC offered £500 for three years for televising just half the game - again the R.L. refused, saying they would not accept less than £1,000 for a telerecording only, not live coverage, so the Wembley showpiece continued not to be televised. But later in 1955, television coverage took a fascinating new turn with the birth of commercial t.v. and the arrival of the nation's second channel - in August 1955 the Rugby League signed a contract with ITV for a floodlit competition which was to be used as a guinea pig for outside broadcasts by the new channel. Eight clubs took part, all receiving £400 each, in a series of midweek floodlit games all played on soccer grounds in London. The final was won by Warrington 43-18 over Leigh, at Loftus Road, the home of Queen's Park Rangers. In marked contrast, the R.L. Council turned down a request from the BBC to televise the 1955 Great Britain versus New Zealand Tests, although a "Rugby League X111" versus the Kiwis Wednesday night floodlit game at Odsal was televised for a £1,000 fee.

After this succession of *ad hoc* relationships with television, by the end of the 1955-56 the R.L. Council was finally given authority to draw up a policy for negotiating more formally with the T.V. companies - the value of the new medium, no doubt, hit home to many of the "doubters" when the accounts of the Northern Rugby League for that season showed a profit of £1,025, but only because a fee of £1,500 had been received from ITV for televising the Championship Final from Maine Road. In October 1957, an ITV offer of £1,000 for a series of eight matches on Saturday afternoons was rejected, but in March 1958 it was agreed that the BBC would televise the Cup Final again, despite subsequent protests from the two finalists Wigan and Workington. By the start of the 1959-60 season, the League had agreed a contract with the BBC to television a minimum of 13 league games on Saturday afternoons, but the concerns resurfaced when the attendance at the deciding Test of the 1959 Ashes series was reduced due to live television. The game wanted T.V., but the controversies were set to rumble on.

(Above)
Programme for the final of the Television Trophy, broadcast by the new commercial channel in 1955. This match won by Warrington against Leigh was played at Queen's Park Rangers Loftus Road ground. The programme cover featured Brian Bevan, describing him as "the Stanley Matthews of Rugby League."

(Above)
Reg Gasnier on his way to a hat-trick of tries in the first Test of the 1959 Ashes series - during which his impact on t.v. viewers was immense.

BARROW

(Above) The Barrow team at Wigan in September 1956, lacking a few of their regular stars like Phil Jackson, Maurice Redhead and Don Wilson. Left to right: *(Standing)*: Frank Castle, Jim Wilson, Bill Healey, Ken Stuart, Dennis Goodwin, Reg Parker, George Woosey. *(Seated)*: Jimmy Lewthwaite, John 'Dinks' Harris, Willie Horne (Captain), Joe Ball, Danny Leatherbarrow and Jack Grundy.

Barrow were one of the teams of 'Fifties, making three Wembley Finals in six years and popular throughout the League for their attractive style, led by the maestro, Willie Horne.

(Left) Willie Horne receives the Cup from Prince Philip at Wembley in 1955.
(Below) An artist's impression of Frank Castle on the run versus Leeds in the 1957 Wembley Final.

(Left) Phil Jackson could claim to be one of the decade's outstanding players, appearing in Barrow's three Wembley Finals, starring as a World Cup winner in 1954 and captaining Great Britain as they sealed the Ashes in 1958 with a record Test win over Australia.

Dave Valentine - first World Cup captain on leading Britain's epic triumph in 1954

*"*We all knew when we got to France for that first World Cup that nobody thought we had a chance. But that wasn't what we, the Great Britain team, thought, or how we felt.

I always felt that it was a good side because we had some very good players - which was one of our main assets. Another thing in our favour was that it was a happy party, and we weren't under any pressure as regards winning the World Cup because everybody gave us no chance - everybody that is but ourselves.

Once we got on the field in France everyone just hit it off together, not one man had a bad game. It just shows what can be done when every man is keen and doing his best.

I don't think that any official Rugby team has ever been sent away to a big match with so little thought given to it. We were conveyed to and from France by motor-coach, and all our travel in France was in the same British coach. That was the only "coach" in the party and my Huddersfield pal and team-mate Billy Banks acted as unofficial trainer, doing the "rubbing down" and looking after the football kit. Welshman Billy was one of the reserves who didn't get to play in any of the matches, but his sense of humour and wise-cracks kept all the lads in great spirits throughout the time we were in France.

Despite being written off when so many of the established internationals were unavailable, I was still hopeful seeing that the players who had joined the team were all so keen - they must have been more than interested to accept selection when some of the "stars" gave backword - and the result proved a success for youth blended with experience.

We had that vital experience in key positions, starting with a very sound full-back in Jim

Dave Valentine becomes the very first captain to lift the World Cup after Britain's victory in Paris in 1954.

Ledgard. Then we had Gerry Helme, who I reckon was the top scrum-half in the world at the time; and I knew I could get the forwards going.

My only worry was whether centre Phil Jackson would be available. Phil was just about at his best then and had been outstanding on the tour to Australia just a few months before. We needed his class and experience in the centre, but he was in the Army and there was some doubt about whether he would be able to go with us.

He didn't travel down in the coach with us from the north of England, but when we got to Dover to catch the ferry there he was, leaning on a lamp post waiting for us. It was misty, he had a trilby on pulled down over his face, and he was standing in the lamplight - it was just like something out of a film.

I'll never forget it because it was such a relief to me. I remember saying to Gerry Helme: *'We're alright now, Phil's here. We'll make them go a bit now.'* We all knew that so much depended on Phil Jackson, and he acted as a kind of lieutenant in the threequarter-line, bringing the best out of young fellows like Mick Sullivan and Davy Rose, my countryman from the Borders.

In my opinion, Gerry Helme was one of the greatest tacticians the game has known. Some of his moves were carried through to the last player, and many involved the ball passing through at least six or seven pairs of hands before the try came. Helme was the key man in our two games against France, in Toulouse and in Paris.

The Rugby League game in southern France is particularly strong, so much so that the spectators and touch-judges, too, are partisan to the last breath. In one game, when Jimmy Ledgard was taking a kick near the touchline, he was grabbed by the jersey and held on the railings.

The World Cup

Paris, 1954

(Above)
The British team celebrate winning the first World Cup Final at the Parc des Princes in Paris, by chairing their captain Dave Valentine and match-winning scrum-half Gerry Helme. The happy players are: David Rose, Ally Naughton, Harry Bradshaw (in civvies), Sam Smith, John Thorley and Basil Watts. Alongside them is the team manager Mr. Gideon Shaw (in overcoat.)

Great Britain's victory in the inaugural World Cup remains one of the most magical moments in the story of Rugby League, as captain Dave Valentine led his team of supposed "no hopers" to a romantic and glorious victory on the most romantic and glorious of stages, the *Parc des Princes* in Paris. The first World Cup competition, staged by France in 1954, was a huge success, producing high quality play and top class sportsmanship which dispelled many pre-tournament fears on the back of Great Britain's controversial tour to Australasia a few months earlier. The Aussies had been reticent about joining in a World Cup, and it was only after the French Rugby League president Paul Barriere and his associates pledged a financial guarantee of £25,000 to cover all travel costs of the visiting teams that Australia agreed to go ahead. Both the Australian and New Zealand teams became the first to fly to Europe, whilst the British travelled to France in a motor coach.

Staging this inaugural World Cup was seen by the French as hugely prestigious, with the games played in impressive stadiums in the major cities of Paris, Toulouse, Marseille, Bordeaux, Lyon and Nantes. Victory in the tournament for France promised to open up many influential political doors to the Rugby League code in their country, but it was not to be thanks to the inspirational leadership of Scotsman Valentine and his brave team.

(Above) **David Rose, Jim Ledgard and Dave Valentine head the team being introduced by manager Gideon Shaw before Britain's win over New Zealand in Boardeaux, with Bill Fallowfield looking on.**

Few gave them a chance as they set out to cross the channel, after a reported 23 players (including seven from the 1954 tour squad) had asked not to be selected, but the new-look Great Britain team rose to every occasion. The 18-man squad consisted of two Scots, two Welshmen and 14 lads from the north of England.

Their opening match against Australia in Lyon provided the first big shock and was to prove crucial - with a young Mick Sullivan making his international debut, Britain beat the Aussies and then went on to draw against favourites France in Toulouse in front of the biggest crowd ever recorded for a Rugby League match in France. Victories for Britain and France on Thursday 11th November, saw the two European nations finish level on points, resulting in a play-off two days later. This first World Cup Final took place on a day of beautiful Autumn sunlight in Paris amid a white-hot atmosphere in the *Parc des Princes*. With Gerry Helme outstanding, Great Britain brilliantly held off a star-studded French team to allow Dave Valentine to become the first man to lift the World Cup, and book a place in history for him and his team.

1954 British squad

Billy Banks (Huddersfield)
Harry Bradshaw (Huddersfield)
Gordon Brown (Leeds)
Bob Coverdale (Hull)
Gerry Helme (Warrington)
Phil Jackson (Barrow)
Frank Kitchen (Leigh)
Jimmy Ledgard (Leigh)
Albert Naughton (Warrington)
Don Robinson (Wakefield T.)
David Rose (Leeds)
Ron Rylance (Huddersfield)
Sam Smith (Hunslet)
Mick Sullivan (Huddersfield)
John Thorley (Halifax)
Dave Valentine (Huddersfield)
Basil Watts (York)
Johnny Whiteley (Hull)
Manager:
Mr. Gideon Shaw (Castleford)

The 1954 World Cup match details

(Above) **Britain's Gordon Brown scores in the 13-all draw with France in Toulouse.**

Saturday 30th October at Parc des Princes, Paris
FRANCE 22 beat NEW ZEALAND 13. Att. 13,240
Sunday 31st October at Stade de Gerland, Lyon
GREAT BRITAIN 28 beat AUSTRALIA 13. Att. 10,250.
Sunday 7th November at Stade Velodrome, Marseille
AUSTRALIA 34 beat NEW ZEALAND 15. Att. 20,000.
Sunday 7th November at Le Stadium Municipal, Toulouse
FRANCE 13 drew with GREAT BRITAIN 13. Att. 37,471.
Thursday 11th November at Stade Municipal, Bordeaux
GREAT BRITAIN 26 beat NEW ZEALAND 6. Att. 14,000.
Thursday 11th November at Stade Malakoff, Nantes
FRANCE 15 beat AUSTRALIA 5.   Att. 13,000
Saturday 13th November at Parc des Princes, Paris - Final
GREAT BRITAIN 16 beat FRANCE 12. Att. 30,368.

The World Cup

The second tournament 1957 - in Australia

(Right)
Great Britain loose-forward Derek Turner in the 31-6 defeat by Australia in 1957, with Kiwi referee Vic Belsham looking on.

1957 British squad

Eric Ashton (Wigan)
Billy Boston (Wigan)
Alan Davies (Oldham)
Jack Grundy (Barrow)
Geoff Gunney (Hunslet)
Tommy Harris (Hull)
Phil Jackson (Barrow)
Lewis Jones (Leeds)
Syd Little (Oldham)
Tom McKinney (St.Helens)
Glyn Moses (St.Helens)
Alan Prescott (St.Helens)
Ray Price (Warrington)
Austin Rhodes (St.Helens)
Jeff Stevenson (Leeds)
Mick Sullivan (Huddersfield)
Derek Turner (Oldham)
Johnny Whiteley (Hull)
Managers:
Mr. Hector Rawson (Hunslet)
Mr. Bill Fallowfield (RFL)

The second World Cup tournament was staged in 1957 in Australia to coincide with the golden jubilee of the Australian Rugby League, and the hosts got the perfect 50th birthday present as centre Dick Poole captained them to the trophy.

Great Britain's mood as they entered the 1957 World Cup could hardly have been more different to the first tournament three years earlier. Britain's 1957 side, captained by Alan Prescott, were hot favourites to win after easily beating the Aussies in the Ashes series at the end of the previous year. But injuries dealt some heavy blows to Great Britain, starting when stand-off Ray Price was injured in a warm up game in Perth and could play no part in the World Cup. Prescott's team beat France comfortably in the opening match in Sydney in front of 50,007 (a record crowd for an Anglo-French encounter) but in their crucial game against Australia two days later, centre Alan Davies was injured early leaving the side to play with 12 men, before Billy Boston also became a passenger for the second-half. A crushing 31-6 defeat was hardly believable for a team regarded as one of the most talented ever to leave British shores, and their woe continued with a shock 29-21 loss to New Zealand. The Aussies beat France to be crowned World Cup winners in a tournament which drew big crowds and provided all four nations with a healthy profit.

The 1957 World Cup match details

(Above) **Great Britain's 1957 World Cup team.**

Saturday 15th June at Sydney Cricket Ground
GREAT BRITAIN 23 beat FRANCE 5. Att. 50,007.
Saturday 15th June at 'The Gabba,' Brisbane
AUSTRALIA 25 beat NEW ZEALAND 5. Att. 29,636.
Monday 17th June at Sydney Cricket Ground
AUSTRALIA 31 beat GREAT BRITAIN 6. Att, 57,955.
Monday 17th June at the Brisbane Exhibition Ground
FRANCE 14 beat NEW ZEALAND 10. Att. 22,142.
Saturday 22nd June at Sydney Cricket Ground
AUSTRALIA 26 beat FRANCE 9. Att. 35,158.
Tuesday 25th June at Sydney Cricket Ground
NEW ZEALAND 29 beat GT. BRITAIN 21. Att. 14,263.
Saturday 29th June at Sydney Cricket Ground
Celebration match - the Winners versus Rest of the World
AUSTRALIA 20 beat THE REST 11. Att. 30,675.

Castleford - when glory days awaited

(*Above*) The Castleford team *circa* 1957-58 - left to right: (*Standing*): Fred Ward, George 'Charlie' Howard, Roland Berry, Frank East, Cliff Burton, Arthur Hattee, John Sheridan. (*In front*): Harry Williams, Barry Walsh, Ron Evans, Ken Pye, Albert Lunn and Jack Boot. It was a time when Cas' were regular strugglers near the bottom of the League - in 1957-58 they finished 29th with only Doncaster below them. But things began to stir after Harry Street was appointed coach, and some glory days awaited for Cas' in the 1960s at Wheldon Road.

Ike set new transfer fee record

(*Above*)
Ike Southward in Oldham colours after breaking the transfer fee record in 1959.

Transfer fees regularly changed hands beween Rugby League clubs throughout the 'Fifties, with activity particularly frenetic every January in the run up to the Challenge Cup signing deadline. It was a regular thing for the League secretary Bill Fallowfield to stay on duty at the Chapeltown Road headquarters in Leeds until midnight on the eve of the deadline, so that last minute signings could be registered in time.

But, although transfers were many, and clubs seemed happy to shell out thousands of pounds to recruit Rugby Union players, the actual transfer-fee record stood unbroken throughout much of the decade.

A new benchmark had been set in 1950-51 when deals involving Joe Egan and Harry Street (both forwards) hit the £5,000 mark, but that record remained un-touched for almost seven years, until Mick Sullivan was signed by Wigan. After Mick had asked for a transfer in October 1957, Huddersfield reluctantly put him on the list at a "prohibitive fee" of £9,500 (nearly twice the existing record) and the Fartown club were mortified when Wigan agree to pay the full amount without quibble.

As the decade neared its close, the five figure barrier was broken when Oldham paid £10,650 to Workington for their international winger Ike Southward in March 1959 - and so Rugby League's record transfer fee had more than doubled during the 'Fifties.

New transfer fee records

1949-50 - ALBERT NAUGHTON - £4,600.
(*From Widnes to Warrington.*)
1950-51 - BRUCE RYAN - £4,750.
(*From Hull to Leeds.*)
1950-51 - JOE EGAN - £5,000.
(*From Wigan to Leigh.*)
1950-51 - HARRY STREET - £5,000.
(*From Dewsbury to Wigan.*)
1957-58 - MICK SULLIVAN - £9,500.
(*From Huddersfield to Wigan.*)
1958-59 - IKE SOUTHWARD - £10,650.
(*From Workington Town to Oldham.*)

Lions on tour - 1950

(Above)
Great Britain captain Ernest Ward offers congratulations to his Australian equivalent Clive Churchill as he hands over the Ashes trophy in 1950. It was the first time in thirty years that the Lions had relinquished the Ashes to Australia.

The RUGBY LEAGUE NEWS

GEO. OLDROYD. Business Manager British Team   TOM SPEDDING. Team Manager British Team

FIRST TEST
AUSTRALIA
v
GREAT BRITAIN

Under the auspices of the
AUSTRALIAN RUGBY LEAGUE
BOARD OF CONTROL.

SYDNEY CRICKET   JUNE 12th
GROUND.   1950.
6d.

With Ernest Ward as captain and Joe Egan the vice-captain both making their second Lions tours, the 1950 Great Britain team were confident they would maintain their country's 30-year grip on the Ashes. But after narrowly losing the third Test in Sydney in the most atrocious conditions, Ernest Ward found himself becoming the first British captain in three decades who had to leave the Ashes behind in Australia.

For the Aussies, captained by full-back Clive Churchill, there was unrestrained delight that their long drought was finally over. Hats were thrown in the air and spectators stayed behind and danced with delight at the Sydney Cricket Ground after the big Australian winger, Ron Roberts, had sprinted to the corner to score the only try of the deciding Test and seal a 5-2 win and the Ashes for the green and golds.

After a week of torrential rain and storms in Sydney, the Cricket Ground pitch had been covered in thousands of tonnes of sand to try to soak up some of the water, leaving quagmire conditions not expected in Australia. The first Test had also been a mudbath, which Great Britain managed to win 6-4 (with two tries from Wigan winger Jack Hilton), but when they got to Brisbane for the second Test, the Lions encountered not only sunny conditions, but also some very controversial refereeing. A local official called Frank Ballard disallowed three tries for Great Britain and also sent off scrum-half Tommy Bradshaw and prop Ken Gee for disputing his "no try" decisions, leaving the Lions with only 11 men. The British team lost this second Test 15-3, and those refereeing decisions were to have a major influence on the rest of the tour and the eventual loss of the Ashes, with Lions manager Mr. George Oldroyd finding himself at the centre of a storm as his team encountered more very questionable refereeing.

Great Britain winger Jack Hilton chases Australia's Noel Pidding at Sydney in the 1950 Ashes.

On a more positive note, the 1950 Lions attracted big crowds everywhere they played, with a new all-time record attendance in Australia of 70,419 being set for the tourists' match against New South Wales in Sydney. This enabled to tour to make an overall profit of £10,350 which, after each player received a bonus of £159, left the Rugby Football League with a profit of £6,213 - an illustration of just how important tours were to the overall welfare of the British game.

Wigan provided a record eight players for the touring team with one of them, Gordon Ratcliffe, a late replacement for Hunslet's Welsh winger Les Williams who withdrew in order to complete his studies at Carnegie College. Skipper Ernest Ward emerged as the leading goal-kicker on the tour with 52, and also top points scorer with 125. The leading try scorer was Salford's former England Rugby Union winger Tom Danby with 34, and Danby also played most games with 18. The tour opened with a fixture in Perth against Western Australia, which the Lions won 87-4. They were to better that scoreline with an 88-nil win versus Central Queensland. Depleted by injuries, the Lions lost both their Test matches in New Zealand.

(Above) **The 1950 Lions, hats and coats on, bags packed and ready to leave - captain Ernest Ward and Ken Traill lead this party of Great Britain players setting out for Australia from Yorkshire, alongside Dewsbury's Harry Street and Roy Pollard.**

TOUR RECORD
In Australia:
Played 19; Won 15; Lost 4.
Lost Test series: 2-1.
In New Zealand:
Played 6; Won 4; Lost 2.
Lost Test series: 2-0.
Tour totals:
Played 25; Won 19; Lost 6.

TEST RESULTS
At Sydney
GB beat AUSTRALIA: 6-4.
At Brisbane
AUSTRALIA beat GB: 15-3.
At Sydney
AUSTRALIA beat GB: 5-2.
At Christchurch
NEW ZEALAND beat GB: 16-10.
At Auckland
NEW ZEALAND beat GB: 20-13.

The 1950 Lions team

Ernie Ashcroft (Wigan)
Tommy Bradshaw (Wigan)
Jack Cunliffe (Wigan)
Arthur Daniels (Halifax)
Tom Danby (Salford)
Joe Egan (Wigan)
Jim Featherstone (Warrington)
Ken Gee (Wigan)
Elwyn Gwyther (Belle Vue R.)
Fred Higgins (Widnes)
Jack Hilton (Wigan)
Willie Horne (Barrow)
Jimmy Ledgard (Leigh)
Harry Murphy (Wakefield)
Dan Naughton (Widnes)

Fred Osmond (Swinton)
Albert Pepperell (Workington)
Doug Phillips (Belle Vue R.)
Roy Pollard (Dewsbury)
Gordon Ratcliffe (Wigan)
Martin Ryan (Wigan)
Bob Ryan (Warrington)
Harry Street (Dewsbury)
Ken Traill (Bradford N.)
Ernest Ward (Bradford N.)
Dickie Williams (Leeds)

Managers:
Mr. George Oldroyd (Dewsbury)
Mr. Tom Spedding (Belle Vue R.)

Lions on tour - 1954

(Above)
The 1954 Lions tour squad pictured on a rooftop in London, at a farewell event with Rugby League officials on the eve of the team's departure by air for Australia.

Captained by Dickie Williams with Ernie Ashcroft his vice-captain, the 1954 Lions tour ran into numerous controversies - yet still managed to produce much free flowing football and a thrilling climax to a very close Ashes series in Australia. The controversies centred on problems with refereeing and Aussie accusations that the tourists used rough-house tactics, with the worst flare-up occuring in a match against New South Wales a week before the final Test in which the referee, Aubrey Oxford, infamously walked off the field and abandoned the game, leaving brawling players to slug it out.

(Above)
Great Britain's Billy Boston and Phil Jackson tackle Aussie centre Harry Wells in the 1954 third Test.

But that did not prevent the Lions proving a big hit at the gate as the tour raised a new record profit of £34,000 for the British Rugby League, a huge increase on the previous best of just over £10,000 in 1950 - with the players being awarded a £400 per man tour bonus.

The 1954 Lions were the first British touring team to fly to Australia - instead of a sea voyage taking over four weeks, Dickie Williams and his men took five days to get to Sydney in what was described as an uncomfortable, and often hair-raising, journey by plane.

A new star was made on the tour with the arrival of Billy Boston on the international scene. At the time he was Britain's youngest tourist, selected after just five first team games for his club, and he went on to be the 1954 tour's top try-scorer with a Lions record of 36. The top goal-kicker was another Welshman, Lewis Jones, with 127 and an individual tally of 278 points which included a record 10 goals in the second Test against Australia at Brisbane. Great Britain had been walloped 37-12 in the opening Test by the Aussies but, with Boston scoring two tries in his Test debut - the table were sensationally

turned in Brisbane to set up a decider on the Sydney Cricket Ground. On a sticky pitch a thrilling encounter unfolded, with Great Britain losing by just four points 20-16, amid complaints that a crucial try under the posts to Aussie centre Harry Wells should not have been allowed because of a double-movement.

The tourists were badly hit by injuries, with Drew Turnbull and Ted Cahill coming home early for operations and Frank Castle only managing to play in five games. At one stage, former Australian Test player Ross McKinnon was called in to help coach the British side, who went on to win the series in New Zealand amid more controversy over alleged rough play.

(Above) **Gerry Helme on the attack for the 1954 Lions in their tour match at Newcastle, with winger Frank Castle in support.**

(Above) **All's well that ends well - wingers Terry O'Grady and Brian Carlson swap jerseys at the end of the series.**

TOUR RECORD

In Australia:
Played 22; Won 13; Lost 7; Drew 1.
Lost Test series: 2-1.
In New Zealand:
Played 10; Won 8; Lost 2.
Won Test series: 2-1.
Tour totals:
Played 32; Won 21; Lost 9; Drew 1.

TEST RESULTS

At Sydney
AUSTRALIA beat GB: 37-12.
At Brisbane
GB beat AUSTRALIA 38-21.
At Sydney
AUSTRALIA beat GB: 20-16.
At Auckland
GB beat NEW ZEALAND 27-7.
At Greymouth
NEW ZEALAND beat GB: 20-14.
At Auckland
GB beat NEW ZEALAND 12-6.

The 1954 Lions team

Ernie Ashcroft (Wigan)
Billy Boston (Wigan)
Jim Bowden (Huddersfield)
Brian Briggs (Huddersfield)
Alf Burnell (Hunslet)
Ted Cahill (Rochdale Hornets)
Frank Castle (Barrow)
Jack Cunliffe (Wigan)
Doug Greenall (St.Helens)
Geoff Gunney (Hunslet)
Tommy Harris (Hull)
Gerry Helme (Warrington)
John Henderson (Workington)
Phil Jackson (Barrow)
Lewis Jones (Leeds)

Tom McKinney (Salford)
Terry O'Grady (Oldham)
Charlie Pawsey (Leigh)
Alan Prescott (St.Helens)
Ray Price (Warrington)
Nat Silcock (Wigan)
Ken Traill (Bradford N.)
Drew Turnbull (Leeds)
Dave Valentine (Huddersfield)
Jack Wilkinson (Halifax)
Dickie Williams (Hunslet)

Managers:
Mr. Hector Rawson (Hunslet)
Mr. Tom Hesketh (Wigan)

Lions on tour - 1958

(Right)
Great Britain's joy on their lap of honour at the Sydney Cricket Ground after the Ashes were retained by thrashing Australia in the third Test in 1958. Injured Lions captain Alan Prescott, his broken arm in a sling, holds the Ashes trophy aloft chaired by Vince Karalius and Mic Sullivan. Others on the picture are: Tom Mitchell (manager), Alan Davies, Ike Southward, Phil Jackson, Eric Fraser and Johnny Whiteley.

N o Lions tour has been the subject of such intense drama and intrigue as the 1958 adventure, which saw Great Britain retain the Ashes in the most sensational style - yet find themselves battling against a split in their camp which became the subject of a Rugby League Council inquest on their return to the U.K.

On the field, the Lions were captained by St.Helens prop Alan Prescott, with Barrow centre Phil Jackson his vice-captain - both were making their second Lions tours after being members of the 1954 side and also playing in Australia in the 1957 World Cup. It quickly became apparent once Prescott's 1958 team got to Australia that there were problems behind the scenes between the managers Bennett Manson and Tom Mitchell, and that coach Jim Brough (the first official coach to travel down-under with a British touring team) was not popular with the players.

The off-field unrest gathered momentum after a poor first Test display which saw Great Britain well beaten in Sydney, meaning it was absolutely vital that they win the second Test to keep the series alive and save the tour. That second Test in Brisbane unfolded as a dramatic battle against the odds to rival the famous "Rorke's Drift" match of 1914 and win its place in the folklore of Rugby League's history. With captain Alan Prescott heroically staying on the field with a broken arm as injuries reduced his side to

(Above)
Alan Prescott, playing with a broken arm, in action against his rival captain Brian Davies in the 1958 Brisbane Test match.

only eight fit men, Great Britain played brilliant football to win 25-18 and square the series in a match forever remembered as "Prescott's Epic."

In the deciding third Test back in Sydney, Phil Jackson captained the Lions to the Ashes with a record breaking 40-17 thrashing of the Aussies. After their defeat in the first Test, the 1958 British side went on to set new records of success with a remarkable unbeaten run which saw the first Test in New Zealand the only game lost in the remaining 22 fixtures on the tour.

(Left)
The Great Britain team of 1958 prepare to board a plane for an internal flight in Australia. Among the group are two well known British newspaper reporters - a youthful Jack McNamara of the *"Manchester Evening News"* at the front holding his portable typewriter, and behind him Phil King of *"The People."*

The British Rugby League made a tour profit of £34,934 with each player receiving £567. Sensational new stars emerged on the tour in players like Alex Murphy, the youngest Lions tourist a 18, and Dick Huddart, who made a record 24 appearances on the tour, scoring 17 tries. Mick Sullivan was top try scorer with a new record of 38 (seven of them scored in the final match against Western Australia in Perth), and Eric Fraser became only the third Lion to kick a century of goals on tour with his total of 110. Winger Ike Southward (one of four Workington Town players in the squad, along with one manager and the coach also from that club) scored 165 points from 25 tries and 45 goals; Leigh's Mick Martyn scored 23 tries, a new tour record for a forward, and Vince Karalius became forever known as "Wild Bull of the Pampas."

TOUR RECORD
In Australia:
Played 21; Won 19; Lost 1; Drew 1.
Won Test series: 2-1.
In New Zealand:
Played 9; Won 8; Lost 1.
Drew Test series: 1-1.
Tour totals:
Played 30; Won 27; Lost 2; Drew 1.

TEST RESULTS
At Sydney
AUSTRALIA beat GB: 25-8.
At Brisbane
GB beat AUSTRALIA: 25-18.
At Sydney
GB beat AUSTRALIA: 40-17.
At Auckland
NEW ZEALAND beat GB: 15-10.
At Auckland
GB beat NEW ZEALAND: 32-15.

The 1958 Lions team

Alvin Ackerley (Halifax)
Harry Archer (Workington)
Eric Ashton (Wigan)
David Bolton (Wigan)
Frank Carlton (St.Helens)
Jim Challinor (Warrington)
Alan Davies (Oldham)
Brian Edgar (Workington)
Eric Fraser (Warrington)
Dennis Goodwin (Barrow)
Tommy Harris (Hull)
Dick Huddart (Whitehaven)
Ken Jackson (Oldham)
Phil Jackson (Barrow)
Vince Karalius (St.Helens)

Mick Martyn (Leigh)
Brian McTigue (Wigan)
Glyn Moses (St.Helens)
Alex Murphy (St.Helens)
Frank Pitchford (Oldham)
Alan Prescott (St.Helens)
Ike Southward (Workington)
Mick Sullivan (Wigan)
Abe Terry (St.Helens)
Johnny Whiteley (Hull)
Bill Wookey (Workington)
Managers:
Mr. Bennett Manson (Swinton)
Mr. Tom Mitchell (Workington)
Coach: Jim Brough (Workington)

Alan Prescott - Great Britain's heroic captain on winning the 1958 Test with a broken arm

"For the rest of my life I could never forget a game like that Test match in 1958 - even if I wanted to, the six inch scar on my right forearm where I had a plate inserted could never let me forget it.

We had played below par in the first Test and got well beaten, so we desperately needed to win the second Test to keep the series alive, otherwise the whole tour would have been a flop. A crowd of 37,000 was packed into the Gabba ground in Brisbane as we walked out, but little did I know that just four minutes later my arm would be in agony.

In the Brisbane casualty ward after the legendary 1958 Test - Alan Prescott and Dave Bolton.

I remember the incident clearly - I went in to tackle Australia's acting half-back Rex Mossop, my arm struck his head and just smashed. It went numb and I knew it was broken. The game was going on around me and I thought to myself *'You can't go off, this Test match has got to be won.'*

I was wondering if I could do any permanent damage when the words of the great Jim Sullivan came to me. I remember Jim, when he was in charge at St.Helens, once saying to us: *'If you are only on the field getting in the way then someone has to beat you. Always stand and face the opposition - never turn your back.'* Those words renewed my determination, I knew I had to stay on.

The first person who knew about my injury was our hooker Tommy Harris. In the fourth scrum, Harris shouted to me: *'The scrum's loose Alan, get tighter.'* I whispered to him so none of the Aussie forwards could hear: *'Sorry Tom, I've broken my arm.'*

Then our centre Jim Challinor collided with the corner flag as he scored and damaged his shoulder. *'I'll have to go off,'* he told me. *'You're joking, I've got a broken arm and you want to go off,'* I replied.

And then the injuries started to pile up.

Stand-off Dave Bolton was taken off with a broken collar bone, full-back Eric Fraser burst a blood vessel in his arm, and loose-forward Vinty Karalius suffered a bruised spine. But we battled on and although we led 10-2 at half-time the dressing room was strangely quiet.

It should have been buzzing, but there were so many injured players that concern had taken over from the excitement of being in front. Only the cocky and confident Alex Murphy stayed relaxed as he stood in front of a mirror combing his brylcreamed hair - that's arrogance for you, but he was having a brilliant game.

An Australian doctor examined my arm and he advised me to stay off the field, warning me that if I continued I could do permanent damage. But I said to Tom Mitchell (the team manager): *'I just can't go off. We would be three men short and we've got to win.'*

Then I saw the look on the faces of the other players. They were watching me, waiting for my reaction. They were ready for the second-half despite being in pain. This made me feel proud - I stood up and shouted: *'Come on lads, let's go out there and destroy these Aussies.'*

We battled through and were overjoyed when we won 25-18. I may have played my part, but every player was magnificent. At the final whistle I ran to Tom Mitchell and screamed: *'We've done it.'* There were tears in my eyes, but it was then that I started to realise how bad my arm was and I became anxious. Facing thirteen Australians with a broken arm didn't bother me, but the thought of an operating table frightened me to death.

When the doctor told me the nature of the break at half-time, I knew we needed a miracle to battle through. That miracle came in the shape of a tremendous surge of patriotic feeling by the players. They did our country proud and it was a moving occasion.

Whitehaven's Cup drama in 1957

(Above) **Whitehaven full-back John McKeown in possession against Hunslet in the second round Cup tie of 1957, the Hunslet defenders are winger Alan Snowdon (number 2) and stand-off Brian Gabbitas, on the floor.** *(Above, right)* **In the famous Odsal semi-final of 1957, Whitehaven's loose-forward Geoff Robinson gets to grips with his Leeds opposite number Harry Street.**

The sheer desire of clubs to get to a Challenge Cup Final at Wembley - and the excitement and heartbreak generated by Cup campaigns - was never better illustrated than Whitehaven in 1957. In their ninth season in the Rugby League, the Cumbrians - eager to emerge from the shadow of their successful neighbours up the coast at Workington - went so close to achieving their Wembley ambition after a Cup campaign that was as dramatic as they come.

The symbolism of teams battling through the worst weather mid-winter could throw at them, inspired by the dream of being able to walk out onto Wembley's lush turf in the spring sunshine, was never enacted more graphically than in Whitehaven's case in 1957. That dream was to end in the most heartbreaking circumstances when a late drop-goal by Leeds scrum-half Jeff Stevenson brought a one point defeat in the semi-final at Odsal Stadium. That semi-final, that one little point, and that drop-goal are still remembered in Whitehaven, over half a century later, as the most significant moment in the club's history.

To get through to the semi-final Whitehaven had enjoyed three home draws in the earlier rounds of the Cup. Their epic run started with a 9-8 win over the actual Cup holders St.Helens, followed by a 7-nil defeat of Hunslet on a day when the weather was so cold that, in the face of a freezing gale, some Hunslet players had to be revived with brandy at half-time after suffering mild hypothermia. In the quarter-final, in pouring rain and on a sodden pitch, Widnes were beaten by a John McKeown penalty-goal, 2 -0, with over 13,500 spectators packed into the Recreation Ground. For the semi-final, six special trains took Whitehaven fans to Bradford where they swelled a crowd of 49,094, by far the biggest the small town Cumbrian club had ever played in front of. That was the magic of the Cup fever generated in the 'fifites.

(Above)
The programme from the 1957 Cup semi-final at Odsal, which saw Leeds beat Whitehaven 10-9, thanks to a late, late drop-goal by Jeff Stevenson. A crowd of over 49,000 watched this most agonising of dramas unfold.

European Championship

(Right)
England back-rowers Charlie Pawsey and Billy Blan force the Other Nationalities winger Lionel Cooper into touch during the "visitors" 31-12 win at Fartown in October, 1952. The Englishman in the background is a young Mick Scott from Hull.

The European International Championship in Rugby League took on a new and exciting dimension when the Other Nationalities team entered the fray in the 1949-50 season. The "Other Nats" playing in their green jerseys, immediately became a big attraction for the fans, and tough opponents for England, France and Wales. Offering the chance to play internnational football for top class Australian players "in exile"- notably: Lionel Cooper, Pat Devery and Johnny Hunter of Huddersfield; Brian Bevan and Harry Bath (Warrington), Arthur Clues (Leeds, later Hunslet) and the Workington Town duo Tony Paskins and Johnny Mudge; the Other Nationalities were always a star-studded outfit, boosted by having Huddersfield's great Scottish loose-forward Dave Valentine at the back of their scrum.

With France at their peak in the early 'fifties, and playing their home games before huge crowds in Marseille and Bordeaux, the Championship was always colourful and full of exciting dramas - not least when the French forwards locked horns with Arthur Clues of the Other Nationalites and sparks flew. Arthur's feud with the French second-rower Eduoard Poncinet

(Above) The England team which beat Wales 35-11 at St.Helens on Tuesday 19th September, 1951, in front of a crowd of 20,918. Left to right: (Standing): Charlie Pawsey, Les White, Billy Blan, Vince McKeating, Mick Scott, Ken Gee, Ernie Ashcroft, Stan McCormick. (Seated): Eppie Gibson, Jack Cunliffe, Jimmy Ledgard (capt.), Alf Burnell, Geoff Tullock and J. Milne (masseur).

(Above) **France v Wales at Marseille in April 1951, with Welsh winger Les Williams (Hunslet) on his way to a try.**

produced the most infamous of all European Championship games, the "Battle of the Boulevard" at Hull in November, 1951. Clues was knocked out by Poncinet straight from the kick-off, but a hat-trick of tries by their captain Lionel Cooper saw the Other Nationalities win 17-14 in their greatest victory. The European Championship was always close, with the title winners decided only on points difference for the first four seasons. The last such Championship, in 1955-56, saw the end of the Wales team, with Welsh players instead included in the "Other Nationalities" side, as they walloped both England and France to be crowned Champions.

(Above) **Arthur Clues was a pivotal figure in the Other Nationalities team through all the years of the European Championship. Here Arthur grapples with England's Mick Sullivan at Wigan in 1955, watched by Reg Parker of England and Welshman John Thorley playing for the 'Others.'**

European Championships in the 'Fifties

1949-50
England 7, Other Nationalities 13. *(at Workington)*
Wales 5, Other Nationalities 6. *(at Abertillery)*
Wales 16, France 8. *(at Swansea)*
France 5, England 13. *(at Bordeaux)*
France 8, Other Nationalities 3. *(at Marseille)*
England 11, Wales 6. *(at Wigan)*
Champions: ENGLAND

1950-51
Wales 4, England 22. *(at Abertillery)*
England 14, France 9. *(at Headingley)*
France 16, Other Nationalities 3. *(at Bordeaux)*
Wales 21, Other Nationalities 27. *(at Swansea)*
England 10, Other Nationalities 35. *(at Wigan)*
France 28, Wales 13. *(at Marseille)*
Champions: FRANCE

1951-52
England 35, Wales 11. *(at St.Helens)*
Other Nationalities 17, France 14. *(at Hull)*
France 42, England 13. *(at Marseille)*
Wales 11, Other Nationalities 22. *(at Abertillery)*
France 20, Wales 12. *(at Bordeaux)*
England 31, Other Nationalities 18. *(at Wigan)*
Champions: FRANCE

1952-53
England 19, Wales 8. *(at Wigan)*
England 12, Other Nationalities 31. *(at Huddersfield)*
Wales 22, France 16. *(at Headingley)*
France 10, Other Nationalities 29. *(at Marseille)*
France 13, England 15. *(at Parc des Princes, Paris)*
Wales 18, Other Nationalities 16. *(at Warrington)*
Champions: OTHER NATIONALITIES

1953-54
England 24, Wales 5. *(at St.Helens)*
Other Nationalities 30, Wales 5. *(at Bradford)*
France 10, Other Nationalities 15. *(at Bordeaux)*
England 7, France 5. *(at Bradford)*
England 30, Other Naionalities 22. *(at Wigan)*
France 23, Wales 22. *(at Marseille)*
Champions: ENGLAND

Tournament not staged in 1954-55 due to World Cup

1955-56
England 16, Other Nationalities 33. *(at Wigan)*
Other Nationalities 32, France 19. *(at Leigh)*
France 23, England 9. *(at Lyon)*
Champions: OTHER NATIONALITIES

Union internationals in League

Several of Rugby League's biggest stars during the 1950s had joined the game from Rugby Union, not least among them the young men from Cardiff, Billy Boston and Johnny Freeman, who became prolific try-scorers and crowd pleasers after "going north." With the transfer-ban in place throughout the decade preventing English clubs signing ready-made Rugby League players from Australia or New Zealand, the search for new blood invariably took them to Rugby Union. Among the Australian "wallaby" internationals recruited by English clubs in the early 'fifties were Trevor Allan and Rex Mossop (to Leigh), Bevan Wilson (to Workington) and Neville Emery (to Whitehaven); whilst the latter part of the decade would see the influx of South Africans, led by Springbok international Tom van Vollenhoven.

(Above)
Lewis Jones in action for Great Britain in New Zealand during the 1954 tour, on which Jones became a dual code British Lion.

But whilst so many Union signings were excellent players in Rugby League during the 'fifties, the number of international caps from the home nations crossing the great divide between the two codes was actually less than the number who would follow in the 1960s. There were 16 Union internationals who joined Rugby League clubs in the 1950s *(as listed below.)* In most cases, the men who had won most caps in Rugby Union, proved to be the least successful in League - notably Robin Thompson, Donald Hayward and Russell Robins, who all numbered caps over double-figures for their home countries and also played Tests for the British Lions (Thompson actually captaining the 1955 Lions to South Africa.) The success stories included David Rose, who had won seven caps for Scotland before joining Huddersfield and, within 12 months, was starring as a World Cup winner; and Garfield Owen, the incumbent Wales full-back when he signed for Halifax. The biggest signing was Lewis Jones leaving Llanelli for Leeds, from whom he received a record £6,000 fee - Lewis was the "golden boy" of Welsh rugby and had played for the British Lions.

Home nations R.U. internationals signed in the 'fifties

England
Tom Danby - signed by Salford, 1949-50
(Harlequins - 1 cap)
Jack Hancock - signed by Salford, 1955-56
(Newport - 2 caps)
Martin Regan - signed by Warrington, 1956-57
(Liverpool - 12 caps)

Ireland
Sean Quinlan - signed by Oldham, 1958-59
(Blackrock & Highfield - 4 caps)
Robin Thompson - signed by Warrington, 1956-57
(Instonians - 11 caps, plus 3 British Lions)

Scotland
Hugh Duffy - signed by Salford, 1954-55
(Jedforest - 1 cap)
David Rose - signed by Huddersfield, 1953-54
(Jedforest - 7 caps)

Wales
Ray Cale - signed by St.Helens, 1950-51
(Pontypool - 7 caps)
Terry Cook - signed by Halifax 1950-51
(Pontypool & Cardiff - 2 caps)
Don Devereux - signed by Huddersfield, 1957-58
(Neath - 3 caps)
Colin Evans - signed by Leeds, 1959-60
(Pontypool - 1 cap)
Donald Hayward - signed by Wigan, 1954-55
(Newbridge - 15 caps, plus 3 British Lions)
Lewis Jones - signed by Leeds, 1952-53
(Llanelli - 10 caps, plus 3 British Lions)
Garfield Owen - signed by Halifax, 1956-57
(Newport - 6 caps)
Russell Robins - signed by Leeds,1958-59
(Pontypridd - 13 caps, plus 4 British Lions)
Brian Sparks - signed by Halifax, 1957-58
(Neath - 7 caps)

BLACKPOOL GAZETTE & HERALD

FYLDE NEWS & ADVERTISER   BLACKPOOL TIMES

No. 7341.   Est. 1843.   FRIDAY, MARCH 8, 1957.   ★ ★   3d.   Tel. 23451.

Lionel Emmitt   Bill Foden   Peter Fearis   Wally McArthur   Jack Brennan   Terry Dunn   Stan Davies   Gilly Wright   Jim Mundy   Ron Fisher   Jim Walsh   Tom Grundy

Sir Frederick Emery, JP, president of Blackpool Borough RL Club, is seen with his son, Mr. R. G. Emery (left), chairman, chatting to Borough players Stan Davies (fullback) and Jim Walsh (captain) and Wally McArthur (winger), right.

"Giant killers" tough test
LEIGH will BRING 7,000

Roy Thornley   Ron Ryder   Charlie Armitt

NEARLY 7,000 people out of the 48,000 population of Leigh are expected in Blackpool tomorrow.

They will be here to watch the Rugby League Cup quarter-final game between Blackpool Borough, "Babes" of the Rugby League, and Leigh, an old-established Lancashire club, writes Jim Nicholson.

Two special trains have been booked bringing 1,800 Leigh fans, and another train is being held in reserve.

All available motor-coaches in Leigh have been booked and many coach owners have had to go out of the town to hire extra

will field the side which beat mighty Oldham, the team fancied for the cup.

The teams will be:

For sale—

OF Blackpool's 5,000 boardinghouses approximately 500, or one tenth, are for sale.

Auctioneers and estate agents made this claim yesterday but added that this had been the position over the past four years.

Very few are selling, too. One firm reported that of their 120 "for sale" boardinghouses they had sold none for the past six months.

The reason for the sales, says Mr. J. Davenport, secretary of the Blackpool Hotel and Boardinghouse Association, is that owners who bought when prices were at £1,000 a bedroom were

Blackpool Borough's Cup fever

The crowd-pulling power of the Challenge Cup was a massive feature throughout the 1950s, and it was quite dramatic how clubs who were struggling to get a few thousand spectators for their weekly league fixtures would be overwhelmed by huge crowds eagerly wanting to see their Cup-ties - such was the lure of Wembley.

The phenomenon of Cup fever was perfectly illustrated by the young Blackpool Borough club in 1957 when, in only their third season in the game, they got through to the quarter-final following two fine away victories at Rochdale and Wakefield in the first two rounds. Drawn at home to Leigh, the seaside resort of Blackpool was caught up in the excitement. The Borough's home stadium at St.Anne's Road was way too small to cater for public demand, so they turned to their Blackpool footballing neighbours and

were granted permission to stage the game at their Bloomfield Road ground. Printed *(above)* is the front page from the local *"Evening Gazette"* newspaper in Blackpool on the eve of the game - it reports on how Leigh anticipated bringing 7,000 fans with them (out of a population of 48,000) with two special trains booked and a third being held in reserve. Plus, every available motor coach - almost 100 - was booked. The report said: *"Cup-tie fever has already gripped the "faithful" few thousand Borough fans, but some thousands of soccer followers are expected to give their support."*

Front page headlines, and daylight training for ther players, meant "the babes" of Blackpool Borough had never had it so good. An official attendance of 20,946 (estimated at over 22,000) turned out at Bloomfield Road, where Leigh ended the fairy-story with a 24-13 victory.

Great Britain's home Tests

Throughout Rugby League's history, going on tour with the Lions to do battle for the Ashes so far from home has always been regarded as the pinnacle of the international game. But the defence of those Ashes on home soil was equally important, albeit without the romance of the mighty Test dramas fought out in Sydney and Brisbane.

During the 'fifties, Great Britain played five home Test series against Australia and New Zealand, and won every one. Of the 15 Test matches contested against our "colonial visitors" (as they were often described back then) Great Britain lost only four. In only one series did the British team have to come back from being one Test down, and that was against the 1959 Australians. Just four different grounds were used to host those Test matches: Swinton, Bradford, Leeds and Wigan, with only Station Road a venue in every series. The biggest attendance was the 37,475 at Odsal Stadium to see the first Test versus New Zealand in 1951. Britain had 11 different captains during the 1950s, with the list *(below, left)* including World Cup games as well as Test matches. Alan Prescott was by far the most prolific British international captain with 17 games in charge, stretching from his debut as skipper at home to New Zealand in 1955 to the fateful day in Brisbane in 1958 when a broken arm ended his Test career.

(Above) **Willie Horne leads Great Britain out for the 1952 first Test, alongside Australia's Clive Churchill.** *(Far right)* **Dickie Williams, captained Great Britain in five Tests in the '50s**

Great Britain 1950s Test match captains

17 - **Alan Prescott** (St.Helens)
5 - **Ernest Ward** (Bradford Northern)
5 - **Dickie Williams** (Leeds & Hunslet)
4 - **Dave Valentine** (Huddersfield)
3 - **Willie Horne** (Barrow)
3 - **Ernie Ashcroft** (Wigan)
3 - **Eric Ashton** (Wigan)
2 - **Phil Jackson** (Barrow)
2 - **Jeff Stevenson** (York)
1 - **Jack Cunliffe** (Wigan)
1 - **Johnny Whiteley** (Hull)

(Above) **The Great Britain team which rescued the Ashes in 1959 by winning the second Test at Headingley. Left to right:** *(Standing):* **Jim Challinor (reserve), Bill Fallowfield (manager), Abe Terry, Brian McTigue, Don Robinson, Johnny Whiteley, Neil Fox, Ike Southward, Dick Huddart (reserve).** *(In front):* **Don Vines, Frank Dyson, Mick Sullivan, Jeff Stevenson (captain), Tommy Harris, Eric Ashton and David Bolton.**

(Left)
Geoff Gunney on his way to a try under the posts at Headingley in the very first match between Great Britain and France to be granted full Test status in January 1957. The Hunslet forward has close support from Lewis Jones as the British team ran out easy winners 45-12, scoring 8 tries in the process, whilst the Welshman Jones kicked nine goals.

(Above) French forward Jean Pambrun passes despite the attention of Great Britain's Don Robinson and David Rose in the 1954 World Cup Final in Paris. The success of this Franco-British clash encouraged the granting of full Test match status to Great Britain versus France games.

The decision to abandon the European Championship and replace it with an annual Test series between Great Britain and France was taken in the 1956-57 season. Fears over the continuing strength of the Welsh and Other Nationalities teams, along with the fact that France was already playing (and winning) Tests against Australia and New Zealand, were major factors in that decision. So, from January 1957, Great Britain playing France was granted full Test status - and, suddenly, the British team appeared to take playing the French far more seriously to dominate the early years of these Test matches. Despite the eccentricities of French referees, it took France eight attempts before they beat Great Britain in a full Test - in the very last encounter of the 'fifties played at Grenoble. Prior to 1957, five Great Britain-France internationals had been played, but without full Test status - which was sad for the many fine players who represented their country in these games but were denied the honour of being awarded a cap.

Great Britain - France matches in the 'Fifites

Pre - full Test status

1952 - 22nd May, at Parc des Princes, Paris.
France 22, Great Britain 12.
1953 - 24th May, at Stade de Gerland, Lyon.
France 28, Great Britain 17.
1954 - 27th April, at Odsal Stadium, Bradford.
Great Britain 17, France 8.
1955 - 11th December, at Parc des Princes, Paris.
France 17, Great Britain 5.
1956 - 11th April, at Odsal Stadium, Bradford.
Great Britain 18, France 10.

Test matches

1956-57 season:
1957 - 26th January, at Headingley, Leeds.
Great Britain 45, France 12.
1957 - 3rd March, at Le Stadium, Toulouse.
France 19, Great Britain 19.
1957 - 10th April, at Knowsley Road, St.Helens.
Great Britain 29, France 14.
1957-58 season:
1957 - 3rd November, at Le Stadium, Toulouse.
France 14, Great Britain 25.
1957 - 23rd November, at Central Park, Wigan.
Great Britain 44, France 15.
1958 - 2nd March, at Stade Municipal, Grenoble.
France 9, Great Britain 23.
1958-59 season:
1959 - 14th March, at Headingley, Leeds.
Great Britain 50, France 15.
1959 - 5th April, at Stade Municipal, Grenoble.
France 24, Great Britain 15.

Gazette through the 'Fifties

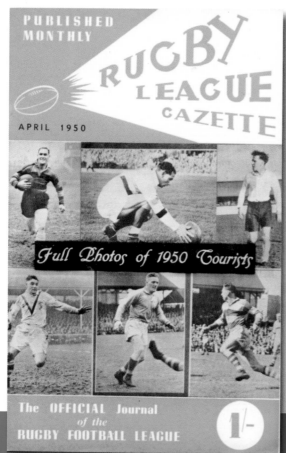

Always colourful and lively, these covers show the *"Rugby League Gazette"* magazine in four of its several different formats during the 1950s.

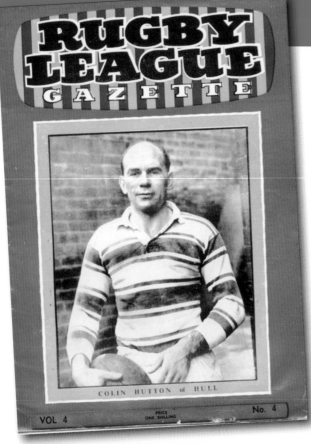

Adams images of the stars

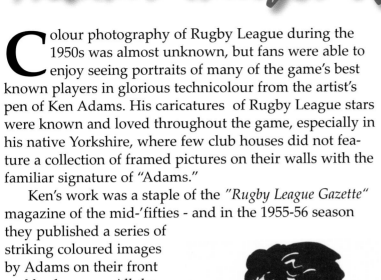

Colour photography of Rugby League during the 1950s was almost unknown, but fans were able to enjoy seeing portraits of many of the game's best known players in glorious technicolour from the artist's pen of Ken Adams. His caricatures of Rugby League stars were known and loved throughout the game, especially in his native Yorkshire, where few club houses did not feature a collection of framed pictures on their walls with the familiar signature of "Adams."

Ken's work was a staple of the *"Rugby League Gazette"* magazine of the mid-'fifties - and in the 1955-56 season they published a series of striking coloured images by Adams on their front and back covers. All the caricatures reprinted on this page are from that series, and they illustrate perfectly the artistic talent of Ken Adams as they give a glimpse of the instantly recognisable features of some of the game's best known stars, as well as the equally distinctive club colours of their various teams. "Adams" brought colour and a smile to the game.

All drawn by Adams - familiar faces of stars of the mid-'fifties in their club colours:
Jeff Stevenson,
Alan Davies,
Don Robinson,
Ted Cahill and
Cec Thompson.

American All Stars adventure

Of all the quirky international adventures Rugby League saw during the 'fifties, nothing was quite so outrageous as the American All Stars who toured Australia and New Zealand in 1953. It was a symbol of the entrepreneurial sprit that was so prevalent in Rugby League at the time that the All Stars tour became a reality after Harry Sunderland had sown the seeds for it in California in 1950, but the naivity of the exercise would be hard for 21st Century sports administrators to believe.

(Above)
Six of the American Allstars of 1953 arrive on the tarmac at Sydney airport. Their manager Mike Dimitro is at the front with the ball, and the others standing are: Al Kirkland, Sol Nauma, Xavier Mena, Bob van Doren and Harold Han.

The driving force behind the American All Stars tour was their manager Mike Dimitro, a former golden gloves boxer, wrestler and gridiron footballer, who was actually a wrestling promoter when he set about putting together a team of players who were a mixture of U.S. College footballers, wrestlers and track athletes. The one thing they had in common was that none of them had ever seen, let alone played, a game of Rugby League. Yet the Australian Rugby League set out a tour of 18 fixtures for the Americans, following the traditional tour path through all parts of New South Wales and Queensland including big games against both State teams, which was followed by eight games in New Zealand. Now, almost 60 years later, it seems incredible to think a team of absolute novices could be expected to be competitive against top profressional players, including Australia's Test stars - but the Aussies were still on the high from the flame that had been lit in their country by the Frenchmen of 1951, and as a spin-off from that there was enormous public interest, intially at least, in the All Stars.

Their flashy red, white and blue stars-and-stripes outfits added to the glamourous aura - and they wore their American Gridiron style long pants for the first two games before changing to normal rugby shorts for the rest of the tour. The All Stars played their first game on 26th May 1953, in Canberra, and incredibly won 34-25. Interest was such that when they lined up against

(Above)
The American Allstars in their match against Sydney, which drew a near sell-out crowd of 65,453 to the Sydney Cricket Ground

Sydney five days later at the Cricket Ground, a crowd of 65,453 was waiting to see them. The penny quickly dropped that they were novices, as the match ended 52-25 to the Sydney team; but still another 32,554 turned up the following week to watch the Americans play New South Wales. A 62-41 scoreline confirmed to many that the tour was a "farce," but as the Yanks travelled around the country areas - with coaching from Aussie Latchem Robinson and the help of one or two guest players, they proved very competitive against experienced and determined opponents, eager to claim the scalp of a visiting international team. The Americans only managed one more victory in their 18 games in Australia, but - and this shows their potential as high quality athletes - that was against the Rugby League stronghold of Newcastle. In New Zealand, the All Stars won three of their eight fixtures. Later in 1953, another American All Stars team (of largely different players) travelled to France and played a five match tour, culminating in an international against the full strength French team in Paris, which the Americans lost 31-0.

Italy takes up Rugby League

(Left)
The Italians tackle Wigan in their first game on British soil, at Central Park on 26th August 1950. A crowd of 14,000 came out to watch them.
(Below)
The Italian players are introduced to the Mayor of Wigan before their debut.

Italy offered Rugby League the hope of establishing a new European stronghold during the 'fifties, starting in 1950 when an Italian team, led by 38-year-old former Rugby Union international Vincenzo Bertoletto, came to Britain and played a six-match tour. Just like Jean Galia's French pioneers in 1934, the Italians made their debut against Wigan at Central Park. 14,000 fans cheered them on, but a 49-28 defeat showed they were well out of their depth against top professional sides as they went on to lose all five subsequent fixtures against: St.Helens, Huddersfield, Leigh, Leeds and a South Wales X111. Bertoletto's team were effectively a Turin club side and, on their return from the tour, they managed to spread the game to Milan.

Several matches were played against French club teams and by April 1951, the first Amateur international between Italy and France was staged at Cahors, with the Italians losing 29-17. A year later, in Turin, Italy got closer with an 18-22 loss to France, and then in 1953 at Perpignan it was just a close, the French winning 22-17. It said much for the Italians' potential that they were so competitive with what was a very able French team, and this continued when Italy went down 20-6 to France and 18-11 to England in an Amateur International tournament played in Yorkshire at Easter 1954. These games were part of another seven match tour to England in which the Italians also were beaten by five professional clubs: Bradford Northern, York, Hunslet, Keighley and Leigh.

A far bigger iniative occurred in Italy, starting in 1958, when the former Wigan player Toni "Rossi" alerted the British Rugby League to the fact that, due to great satisfaction with the Rugby Union, the whole of the Venito region had switched to the 13-man game. This region was the stronghold of Italian rugby, including Venice, Padua, Treviso and Verona. Bill Fallowfield was very supportive of the Italians and acted quickly to ensure the British League offered assistance, both financial and with coaching. An Italian Rugby League was officially founded on 13th September 1958, with 21 clubs in membership, and their enthusiasm was tremendous as the end of the decade approached.

The Rugby Football League

Amateur International Tournament

FRANCE v. ITALY
At FARTOWN, HUDDERSFIELD
FRIDAY, 16th APRIL   Kick-off 6.30 p.m.

ENGLAND v. FRANCE
At HEADINGLEY, LEEDS
SATURDAY, 17th APRIL   Kick-off 3 p.m.

ENGLAND v. ITALY
At THRUM HALL, HALIFAX
MONDAY, 19th APRIL   Kick-off 3 p.m.

Official Programme . . 3d.

(Above)
Programme for the Amateur Internationl tournament in 1954 in which Italy played valiantly against both England and France.

The most sensational tour

The date was 21st July 1951, as Puig-Aubert was carried aloft by his joyous team-mates around the Sydney Cricket Ground. Paul Bartoletti and Martin Martin are chairing their skipper, as Jo Crespo, Vincent Cantoni, Jean Duhau (coach) and Gaston Calixte join the group. They had just administered a footballing lesson to Australia on their own turf, winning the third Test 35-14 to put the seal on the 1951 French team's unforgettable debut tour - which is still remembered as the most sensational tour Rugby League has ever seen.

(Left)
The 1951 French touring pictured at the Sydney Cricket Ground. Captain Robert Caillou sits in the middle, flanked by Rene Duffort and Puig Aubert, with manager Antoine Blain standing directly behind him and scrum-half Jean Dop holding the ball in front of him. The coaches, Bob Samatan and Jean Duhau sit at each end of the row.

People in Australia still talk about the 1951 French team. A new dimension was added to international Rugby League when France made their first southern-hemisphere tour, under the captaincy of Robert Caillou and guidance of manager Antoine Blain. They were the first team to fly to Australia and, as they embarked from the airport at Marseille, there were many nervous concerns about how they would cope with the Aussies on their own grounds. Financing the tour was a huge gamble by the French Rugby League's leading officials, Paul Barriere and Claude Devernois - but it paid off in spectacular style.

In their colourful tricolour uniforms, the French team won the hearts of the Australian crowds as they played a razzle-dazzle style of rugby which ran the home teams off their feet. The biggest star of all was the full-back Puig-Aubert (nicknamed *Pipette* due to his liking for cigarettes) who broke the long held tour points-scoring record of Jim Sullivan. Other stars were the jack-in-a-box scrum-half Jean Dop; the mighty second-row pairing Elie Brousse and Eduoard Poncinet; wingers Cantoni and Contrastin; and the hot-headed prop Louis "Lo-lo" Mazon. This 1951 French team beat Australia in the first Test at Sydney; lost the second at Brisbane; and then proceeded to humiliate the Aussies (who had won the Ashes from Great Britain the previous year) in the decider, France winning 35-14. The excitement followed the French across the Tasman where they lost their one Test match to the Kiwis in the most controversial game ever seen in New Zealand. The team who had slipped out of France nervously and without fanfare, were welcomed back to a ticker-tape procession through the streets of Marseille watched by as many as 100,000 people - while Puig Aubert became the most famous sports personality in France for 1951.

Four years later, the French returned to Australasia, their 1955 touring team captained by Jackie Merquey. They played to even bigger crowds and - once again - beat Australia in the Test series on their own turf.

(Above)
Second-rower Eduoard Poncinet gets to grips with Johnny Hawke of Australia in the 1951 third Test.

1951 TOUR RECORD
First game: 23rd May 1951, at Canberra.
Last game: 26th August 1951, at Perth.
In Australia:
Played 21; Won 15; Drew 3; Lost 3.
Won Test series: 2-1.
In New Zealand:
Played 7; Won 6; Lost 1.
Lost sole Test match.
1955 TOUR RECORD
First game: 15th May 1955, at Perth.
Last game: 15th August 1955, at Auckland.
In Australia:
Played 25; Won 15; Lost 10.
Won Test series: 2-1.
In New Zealand:
Played 8; Won 4; Lost 4.
Drew Test series: 1-1.

Puig-Aubert - France's most famous player on his sensational tour to Australia in 1951

"As a Rugby player I could only ever conceive a game based on attack, and I think that our 1951 French team proved in Australia that unothodox attack pays. We never played the 'close' or 'tight' game and that was the reason why we won nearly all our matches easily enough and beat Australia in the Test series - by playing an 'open' game and concentrating on rapid passing of the ball.

Puig-Aubert kisses the Franco-Australian trophy after victory at Sydney in 1951, with French trainers Bob Samatan and Jean Duhau plus manager Antoine Blain.

Australians were shocked at our 30 to 40-yard passes from one side of the field to the other, by our overhead passes and passes through the legs. But if they confuse your rivals and you have confidence in their use, why not?

Personally, I never much loved training and I had to be forced to train in spite of the fact that if I had trained conscientiously I would certainly have improved my game enormously - an improvement which I did actually achieve on tour in Australia where, for four months, we lived a well regulated life of strict daily work-outs. This regular, systematic training could not be undertaken back home in France by a *treiziste* (Rugby League player) because the income received from playing had to be augmented by taking a full-time job.

For me the ablity to produce the unexpected always compensated for lack of wind from all those cigarettes I smoked.

When the French team arrived in Australia for our 1951 tour, my old friend and opponent, Clive Churchill, was considered the best back in the world, and even the French players themselves doubted the result of my duel with Churchill. My own confidence, however, never failed me, and every time I met Churchill I think I did just as well as he did, some said better. I learned subsequently from other Australian players that he was tense every time we met on the field, sometimes even sick from nervousness.

My own relaxed attitude was such that, in the first match we played at Sydney and on the occasion of my first kick at goal, after placing the ball - as was my habit - I walked away with my back to the ball and then turned. At that moment I heard the crowd laugh; but happily for me they did not laugh often during my tour of Australia.

For all the French players the matches we won during the 1951 tour were especially prized by us because, on our arrival in Australia, after the victorious 1948 tour of the Kangaroos in France, the press and - as a direct result - the public, did not take us seriously. I remember articles by certain Australian players which described us as 'ballet dancers, champagne swillers,' and so on. For us, this was an excellent incentive to show what we could do, and we beat the Aussies.

The third Test in Sydney, which we won by 35 points to 14, will always remain the most outstanding memory of my long career. We Frenchmen really flipped the ball around and we inspired each other that day. All my life I will remember that parade after the game with the cup to the acclaim of the Sydney public.

Another imperishable memory was our return from Australia to Marseille, where we paraded, each in an open top car, to the applause of some fifty to sixty thousand people, even more loudly cheered than the President of the Republic. Thanks to that victorious tour in 1951, I received the great honour of being named by the famous Parisian sporting paper *'L'Equipe,* the 'Best Sportsman of the Year.'

For all these reasons, the French League's first Australian tour in 1951 remained the greatest memory of my sporting career.

Trinity youngsters beat the Aussies

Wakefield Trinity showed early signs of building the great side they were to become in the 1960s, when their young hopefuls recorded a memorable win over the Australian tourists in 1956. Trinity beat the Kangaroos 17-12 with a team full of up and coming local lads. The Wakefield back division that day was: Ted Wilkins (age 20), Ken Hirst (16), Neil Fox (17), Keith Holliday (21), Fred Smith (20), Ken Rollin (18) and Johnny Bullock (19). The youngest of that group, Ken Hirst, was still a schoolboy and scored a sensational 70-yard try after just two minutes. Another try scorer was stand-off Ken Rollin, pictured *(above)* on the attack for Trinity in another match in the 'Fifties versus Leeds. The group picture *(top, right)* shows the Wakefield Trinity and Australian teams together before kick-off on 10th December 1956.

Dewsbury at Crown Flatt - 1958

(Above) The Dewsbury team in September 1958. Left to right: *(Standing):* Maurice Bamford, Bob Taylor, Gilly Farnell, Ken Pickersgill, Willy O'Donnell, Maurice Cox, Peter Todd. *(In front):* Jack Wilson, Jack Clark, Geoff Popplewell, John Curley, Dave Cox and Ken Bosworth.

All aboard the 'Airlie Bird Express' to Wembley

(Left) In the days of steam, the Hull players pose at the city's Paragon Station in front of the train that was to take them to London for the 1959 Cup Final. Among this group are the players who appeared at Wembley: Arthur Keegan; Stan Cowan, Brian Cooper, Brian Saville, Ivor Watts; George Matthews; Tom Finn, Mick Scott, Tommy Harris, Jim Drake, Cyril Sykes, Bill Drake and Johnny Whiteley.

Kangaroo tours to Europe

1952

(Above)
Captain Clive Churchill and the 1952 Australians before their opening tour game at Keighley.

With the brilliant full-back Clive Churchill at the helm as captain-coach, the 1952 Australian touring team sailed from Sydney aboard the liner *Strathnaver* in July 1952, and returned home in March the following year. They were a relatively humble bunch of Aussies as they arrived in England after being beaten at home by both France and New Zealand in their two most recent Test series, although they did have that rare experience for a Kangaroo team of bringing the Ashes cup with them following the victory of Churchill's team in Australia in 1950.

In their long tour through England and France of 40 matches, this Aussie side emerged with much credit - but no trophies as they lost the Test series in both countries. Willie Horne led Great Britain to convincing wins in the opening two Tests, before Australia turned the tables in the "Battle of Odsal" dead rubber. Across the channel, a thrilling series saw France repeat their 1951 triumph and beat the Aussies on French soil for the first time. Big crowds watched the Kangaroos in both England and France, enabling the Aussies to go home with a healthy profit and a bonus of £332 per man for each player. During their 1952 tour, the Australians encountered television for the first time. Their opening fixture at Keighley was broadcast live by the BBC, and the first Test at Headingley was Australia's first international match to be televised. As well as Churchill, stars on the our included second-rower Brian Davies and young winger Brian Carlson (top try scorer with 29) - both would cross swords with Great Britain in many more Tests during the 'fifties.

1952 Kangaroos in Britain

September		Result		Att.
Sat. 6 -	Keighley	Won	54-4	7,391
Mon. 8 -	Hull	Won	28-0	15,500
Thurs. 11 -	Barrow	Won	26-2	16,044
Sat. 13 -	Whitehaven	Won	15-5	9,301
Mon. 15 -	Oldham	Drew	7-7	19,620
Sat. 20 -	Halifax	Won	39-7	20,000
Wed. 24 -	Wigan	Won	23-13	16,359
Sat. 27 -	St.Helens	Lost	8-26	18,000
October				
Wed. 1 -	Featherstone	Won	50-15	4,000
Sat. 4 -	**GT. BRITAIN (1)**	**Lost**	**6-19**	**34,305**
Wed. 8 -	Bradford N.	Won	20-6	29,287
Sat. 11 -	Warrington	Won	34-10	21,378
Wed. 15 -	Leigh	Won	34-5	8,500
Sat. 18 -	Swinton	Won	31-8	10,269
Wed. 22 -	Hunslet	Won	49-2	3,272
Sat. 25 -	Workington T.	Won	27-15	10,250
Thurs. 30 -	Doncaster	Won	41-13	2,500
November				
Sat. 1 -	Huddersfield	Won	27-9	27,490
Sat. 8 -	**GT. BRITAIN (2)**	**Lost**	**5-21**	**31,358**
Wed. 12 -	Wakefield T.	Won	58-8	6,074
Sat. 15 -	Hull K.R.	Won	31-6	7,000
Wed. 19 -	Lancashire	Won	36-11	5,843
Sat. 22 -	Leeds	Won	45-4	20,000
Wed. 26 -	Yorkshire	Won	55-11	3,737
December				
Wed. 3 -	Dewsbury	Won	22-7	2,405
Sat. 6 -	Widnes	Won	18-7	9,000
Sat. 13 -	**GT. BRITAIN (3)**	**Won**	**27-7**	**30,509**

TOUR RECORD
First game: 6th September 1952, at Keighley.
Last game: 1st February 1953, at Toulouse.
In Britain:
Played 27; Won 23; Drew 1; Lost 3.
Lost Test series: 2-1.
In France:
Played 13; Won 10; Lost 3.
Lost Test series: 2-1.

TEST RESULTS
GT. BRITAIN beat AUSTRALIA 19-6 *(at Leeds)*
GT. BRITAIN beat AUSTRALIA 21-5 *(at Swinton)*
AUSTRALIA beat GT. BRITAIN 27-7 *(at Bradford)*
AUSTRALIA beat FRANCE 16-12 *(at Paris)*
FRANCE beat AUSTRALIA 5-0 *(at Bordeaux)*
FRANCE beat AUSTRALIA 13-5 *(at Lyon)*

The 1956 Kangaroo tour has gone down in history as one of the most disappointing visits by an Australian team to England, although things did look up for the Aussies when they got to France. They were the first Kangaroo touring side to fly to England (although they did travel back home by sea on the liner *Arcadia)* and the decision to delay their arrival until after their own domestic competitions were completed did not help them. It resulted in a much shorter tour with fewer fixtures, and the British Rugby League advised them that not starting the tour until 10th October would mean missing out on light nights for midweek games throughout September, and a subsequent drop in attendances. The shorter tour, and the Aussies' disappointing results - losing nine of their 19 games in England - meant it was not a financial success, with receipts way down on the 1952 tour and the Australian players receiving a miserly bonus of only £90, on top of the £10 per week they were paid on the tour.

From the football point of view, there was a difficult situation for captain-coach Ken Kearney, with Clive Churchill - his predecessor - also included in the side as vice-captain. There were many who thought Churchill should have either been reinstated as captain, or not chosen at all. It proved to be an unhappy tour, with the Aussies conceding the Ashes meekly 19-nil to Great Britain in the deciding Test at Swinton. More sunshine and firmer pitches in France seemed to revitalise the 1956 Kangaroos, and they became the first Australian side to go through France unbeaten.

(Above)
Ken Kearney leads his 1956 Kangaroos out at his old stamping ground of Headingley with Keith Holman immediately behind. Kearney had begun his Rugby League career with Leeds.
(Left)
Great Britain's Geoff Gunney on the attack in the decisive third Test at Swinton, Jack Grundy and Syd Little are in support.

TOUR RECORD
First game: 10th October 1956 at Liverpool.
Last game: 13th January 1957, at Lyon.
In Britain:
Played 19; Won 10; Lost 9.
Lost Test series: 2-1.
In France:
Played: 9; Won 8; Drew 1; Lost 0.
Won Test series: 3-0.
TEST RESULTS
GT. BRITAIN beat AUSTRALIA 21-10 (*at Wigan)*
AUSTRALIA beat GT. BRITAIN 22-9 (*at Bradford)*
GT. BRITAIN beat AUSTRALIA 19-0 (*at Swinton)*
AUSTRALIA beat FRANCE 15-8 (*at Paris)*
AUSTRALIA beat FRANCE 10-6 (*at Bordeaux)*
AUSTRALIA beat FRANCE 26-21 (*at Lyon)*

1956 Kangaroos in Britain

October		Result		Att.
Wed.10 -	Liverpool City	Won	40-12	4,712
Sat. 13 -	Leeds	Lost	13-18	24,459
Mon. 15 -	Hull X111	Won	37-14	17,172
Thurs. 18 -	Barrow	Won	25-11	9,988
Sat. 20 -	Whitehaven	Lost	11-14	10,917
Wed. 24 -	Bradford N.	Won	23-11	2,743
Sat. 27 -	Warrington	Lost	17-21	15,613
Mon. 29 -	N.R.L. X111	Won	19-15	7,811
November				
Sat. 3 -	York	Won	20-18	6,842
Wed. 7 -	Oldham	Lost	2-21	8.458
Sat. 10 -	Huddersfield	Won	20-10	12,127
Sat. 17 -	**GT. BRITAIN (1)**	**Lost**	**10-21**	**22,473**
Wed. 21 -	Hunslet	Won	27-11	4,451
Sat. 24 -	St.Helens	Lost	2-44	15,579
December				
Sat. 1 -	**GT. BRITAIN (2)**	**Won**	**22-9**	**23,354**
Wed. 5 -	Halifax	Lost	3-6	2,254
Sat. 8 -	Wigan	Won	32-4	15,854
Mon. 10 -	Wakefield T.	Lost	12-17	3,381
Sat. 15 -	**GT. BRITAIN (3)**	**Lost**	**0-19**	**17,542**

Kangaroo tours to Europe

(Right)
Reg Gasnier scores one of his hat-trick of tries, leaving Billy Boston in his wake, as the Aussies won the 1959 first Test at a packed Station Road, Swinton.

1959 Kangaroos in Britain

September		Result		Att.
Sat. 12 -	Leeds	Won	44-20	14,629
Tues. 15 -	Rochdale H.	Won	27-14	10,155
Sat. 19 -	Warrington	Won	30-24	17,112
Wed. 23 -	Lancashire	Lost	22-30	15,743
Sat. 26 -	Salford	Won	22-10	11,088
Mon. 28 -	Yorkshire	Lost	15-47	7,359
October				
Thurs. 1 -	Widnes	Won	45-15	9,381
Sat. 3 -	Oldham	Won	25-14	17,630
Wed. 7 -	Leigh	Lost	18-17	11,932
Sat. 10 -	St.Helens	Won	15-2	29,156
Sat. 17 -	**GT. BRITAIN (1)**	**Won**	**22-12**	**35,224**
Thurs. 22 -	Workington/W'haven	Won	13-8	7,463
Sat. 24 -	Barrow	Lost	9-12	8,488
Mon. 26 -	Hull / Hull K.R.	Won	29-9	15,944
November				
Wed. 4 -	Bradford N.	Won	29-8	4,126
Sat. 7 -	Halifax	Won	17-5	8,274
Wed. 11 -	Featherstone R.	Lost	15-23	7,671
Sat. 14 -	Wigan	Lost	9-16	24,466
Sat. 21 -	**GT. BRITAIN (2)**	**Lost**	**10-11**	**30,029**
Wed. 25 -	Swinton	Won	25-24	5,021
Sat. 28 -	Wakefield T.	Lost	10-20	17,615
December				
Wed. 2 -	Huddersfield	Won	21-7	2,349
Sat. 5 -	Hunslet	Won	12-11	8,061
Sat. 12 -	**GT. BRITAIN (3)**	**Lost**	**12-18**	**26,089**

The tenth Kangaroos were led on their journey through Europe by captain Keith Barnes and vice-captain Rex Mossop *(pictured, left)* on what was very much the first of the modern day tours by Australia. So much had changed in the world in the three years since the 1956 Kangaroos' visit, and the 1959 touring team announced on the world stage the arrival of a new breed of young stars like Reg Gasnier, Ken Irvine and Johnny Raper, who were destined to become icons of the 'sixties. The 1959 Kangaroos also gave the strongest possible hint of a changing order in the world of Rugby League and Australia's modern day domination which was to follow.

In the final analysis, the 1959 tourists came within a fraction of becoming the first all Australian team to win the Ashes on British soil, and it was only a couple of centimetres of woodwork at Headingley which denied them an historic series victory. That was because a goal-kick from almost straight in front by Brian Carlson in the second Test hit the post and bounced the wrong way. It was an easy kick, and Carlson was distraught that his miss contributed to a one point defeat for the Aussies - after he had been forced into kicking duties when ace goal-kicker Keith Barnes injured his hamstring earlier in the game. Australia lost 11-10 and the Ashes went to a decisive third Test at Wigan. All this came after the Kangaroos had won the opening Test at Swinton in style, with the young centre Gasnier making a sensational Ashes debut with a hat-trick of tries. Gasnier's speed left

(Above, left) **Captains Jeff Stevenson and Keith Barnes lead their teams out at Headingley for the second Test of the 1959 Ashes series. Behind Barnes is his Kangaroo vice-captain Rex Mossop, whilst in the British line up we see Neil Fox, about to make his Ashes debut.** (Above, right) **Hectic forward action in the third and deciding Test of 1959 at Central Park as Great Britain's Abe Terry and John Whiteley bring to ground Australia's Brian Hambly. In the background are British forwards Tommy Harris and Jack Wilkinson.**

the British defenders grasping thin air, and stamped him immediately as the biggest attraction of the tour. Great Britain, with so many players high on confidence after thrashing the Aussies in 1958, were shell-shocked by their first Test defeat, and wholsesale changes were made to the team for the second Test - a "do or die" encouter at Headingley.

In came Jeff Stevenson as scrum-half and the new captain, after being inspirational in Yorkshire county's incredible 47-15 thrashing of the tourists at Clarence Street, York. It was Stevenson's clever move at the back of the scrum which put Johnny Whiteley over for the decisive try as Britain levelled the series by the narrowest of margins.

Australia lost the deciding Test at Wigan 18-12, despite scoring the game's best two tries, and were left to rue the Ashes series that got away. Their 24 year old captain Keith Barnes, who had emigrated from Wales 12 years earlier, along with Clive Churchill as non-playing coach, were pretty proud at the way their team had come back after the humil- iation Australia had suffered on home soil in the 1958 Ashes series. Just like the 1956 Kangaroos, the 1959 side broke off from their English tour to fly to Paris for the first Test in France on 31st October, where Australia won a thriller 20-19 - and then, after completing the rest of their 11 matches in France, the Kangaroos made history by playing two games in Italy before heading home in late January 1960.

(Above) **Don Fox touches down in Featherstone Rovers' 23-15 win over the 1959 Kangaroos, with the referee Eric Clay in close pursuit.**

TOUR RECORD
First game: 12th September 1959, at Leeds.
Last game: 24th January 1960, at Treviso (Italy.)
In Britain:
Played 24; Won 15; Lost 9.
Lost Test series: 2-1.

In France: **In Italy:**
Played 11; Won 9; Lost 2.   Played 2; Won 2.
Won Test series: 3-0.

TEST RESULTS
AUSRALIA beat GT. BRITAIN 22-14 (at Swinton)
GT. BRITAIN beat AUSTRALIA 11-10 (at Leeds)
GT. BRITAIN beat AUSTRALIA 18-12 (at Wigan)
AUSTRALIA beat FRANCE 20-19 (at Paris)
AUSTRALIA beat FRANCE 17-2 (at Bordeaux)
AUSTRALIA beat FRANCE 16-8 (at Roanne)

The Kiwis came on tour

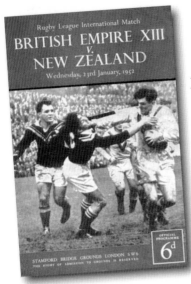

(Above)
The Kiwis ended their tour at Chelsea.

New Zealand came to Europe in 1951 with high hopes, following a series of impressive results on their home soil against France earlier that year and Great Britain in 1950, but they went home empty handed with five defeats in their five Tests. However, they did have the satisfaction of winning many friends with their attractive style of football, and achieving a healthy financial balance for the New Zealand Rugby League after drawing big attendances in both England and France.

Captained by centre Morrie Robertson, the Kiwis gave Great Britain three very close games in the Test matches, and New Zealand were particularly unlucky not to win the second Test at Swinton after British full-back Jimmy Ledgard kicked a last minute penalty goal to obtain a 20-19 victory for the home side. New Zealand had scored five tries to four in this Test which produced a thriller for BBC viewers at home in the first Rugby League match to be televised live in the north of England. Likewise in the third Test, when the Kiwis matched Great Britain four tries apiece, but couldn't kick a goal in their 16-12 loss. That was particularly disappointing for their full-back Des White, who had been one of the stars of the tour as he kicked a new Kiwi tour record of 63 goals in Britain.

(Above) **Tommy Baxter, a star of the 1951 Kiwis, returned in 1955 as their captain.**

There was also a new record for Great Britain when winger George Wilson, a Scotsman, scored tries in all three Tests, including a hat-trick in the first. In the third Test at Leeds, both Britain's wingers were Scots, with Wilson being joined by Drew Turnbull. As well as White, other stand-out players for the Kiwis were Cyril Eastlake, Tommy Baxter and the rugged forward Charlie McBride. The 1951 tourists also played in Wales, against Cardiff, and ended their tour at Chelsea's Stamford Bridge.

1951 Kiwis in Britain

		Result		Att.
September				
Tues. 18 -	Rochdale H.	Won	13-9	4,000
Sat. 22 -	Halifax	Lost	12-18	15,000
Wed. 24 -	Workington T.	Won	17-15	8,935
Sat. 29 -	Oldham	Lost	18-21	15,174
October				
Wed. 3 -	Castleford	Won	10-9	6,600
Sat. 6 -	**GT. BRITAIN (1)**	**Lost**	**15-21**	**37,475**
Wed. 10 -	Huddersfield	Won	34-12	9,859
Sat. 13 -	Warrington	Won	19-13	18,889
Tues. 16 -	Batley	Won	20-13	5,087
Wed. 17 -	Bramley	Won	24-20	2,100
Sat. 20 -	St.Helens	Won	33-10	17,000
Wed. 24 -	Leigh	Won	31-10	9,000
Sat. 27 -	Barrow	Lost	5-9	13,319
Wed. 31 -	Bradford N.	Lost	8-13	29,072
November				
Sat. 3 -	Wigan	Won	15-8	13,500
Wed. 7 -	York	Won	15-12	4,183
Sat. 10 -	**GT. BRITAIN (2)**	**Lost**	**19-20**	**28,246**
Wed. 14 -	Wakefield T.	Won	26-18	8,850
Sat. 17 -	Leeds	Won	19-4	16,000
Thurs. 22 -	Lancashire	Lost	12-13	7,313
Sat. 24 -	Belle Vue R.	Lost	5-7	5,000
Thurs. 29 -	Hull	Won	28-8	9,000
December				
Sat. 1 -	Salford	Won	37-12	10,000
Wed. 5 -	Yorkshire	Won	10-3	2,910
Friday 7 -	Wales (at Odsal)	Won	15-3	8,568
Wed. 12 -	Cardiff	Won	18-10	2,000
Sat. 15 -	**GT. BRITAIN (3)**	**Lost**	**12-16**	**18,649**
January 1952				
Wed. 23 -	Empire X111	Lost	2-26	6,800

TOUR RECORD
First game: 18th September 1951, at Rochdale
Last game: 23rd January 1952, at Chelsea.
In Britain:
Played 28; Won 18; Lost 10.
Lost Test series: 3-0.
In France:
Played 12; Won 7; Drew 1; Lost 4.
Lost Test series: 2-0.
TEST RESULTS
GT. BRITAIN beat N. ZEALAND 21-15 *(at Bradford)*
GT. BRITAIN beat N. ZEALAND 20-19 *(at Swinton)*
GT. BRITAIN beat N. ZEALAND 16-12 *(at Leeds)*
FRANCE beat NEW ZEALAND 8-3 *(at Paris)*
FRANCE beat NEW ZEALAND 17-7 *(at Bordeaux)*

(Left)
New Zealand prop Henry Maxwell dives over for a try in the 1955 first Test at Swinton, despite the attention of British forwards Jack Wilkinson and Peter Foster. The referee, Mr. A. Hill, has a perfect view.

The 1955 New Zealanders were the first Kiwi touring team to fly to England - although they had travelled by air to France for the World Cup the previous year. They broke new ground by opening their tour at the seaside, as the young Blackpool Borough club - in their second season - drew an impressive 12,000 crowd and achieved an even more impressive result of a 24-all draw. The 1955 tourists were the first New Zealand team to play a three match Test series in France, which they lost 2-1 to a confident French team.

Captained by Aucklander Tommy Baxter at centre, the Kiwis lost the series in Great Britain fairly meekly in the first two Tests. New Zealand were poor as they were easily beaten 25-6 at Swinton in the first Test, after which they enlisted the help of their countryman Cec Mounford, the Warrington coach, who certainly improved the Kiwi performances. Their flowing football in the third Test was a sign of what might have been achieved, as they ran riot to score six tries against Great Britain.

TOUR RECORD
First game: 10th September 1955, at Blackpool.
Last game: 21st January 1956, at Paris.
In Britain:
Played 26; Won 13; Drew 2; Lost 11.
Lost Test series: 2-1.
In France:
Played 11; Won 5; Drew 1; Lost 5.
Lost Test series: 2-1.
TEST RESULTS
GT. BRITAIN beat N. ZEALAND 25-6 (*at Swinton*)
GT. BRITAIN beat N. ZEALAND 27-12 (*at Bradford*)
N. ZEALAND beat GT. BRITAIN 28-13 (*at Leeds*)
FRANCE beat NEW ZEALAND 24-7 (*at Toulouse*)
NEW ZEALAND beat FRANCE 31-22 (*at Lyon*)
FRANCE beat NEW ZEALAND 24-3 (*at Paris*)

1955 Kiwis in Britain

September		Result		Att.
Sat. 10 -	Blackpool Boro'	Drew	24-24	12.015
Wed. 14 -	York	Lost	16-20	8,174
Sat. 17 -	Halifax	Lost	17-18	12,492
Wed. 21 -	Yorkshire	Won	33-17	7,907
Sat. 24 -	Wigan	Lost	15-17	19,386
Mon. 26 -	Hull	Won	17-12	10,167
Thurs. 29 -	Barrow	Lost	13-17	7,098
October				
Sat. 1 -	Workington T.	Won	26-16	11,043
Sat. 8 -	**GT. BRITAIN (1)**	**Lost**	**6-25**	**21,937**
Wed. 12 -	Lancashire	Won	17-15	6,887
Sat. 15 -	Leeds	Won	18-16	15,738
Wed. 19 -	Featherstone R.	Won	7-6	5,100
Sat. 22 -	Huddersfield	Lost	16-25	11,271
Wed. 26 -	St.Helens	Lost	8-16	14,000
Sat. 29 -	Oldham	Won	15-13	15,000
November				
Wed. 2 -	Leigh	Lost	13-14	3,400
Sat. 5 -	Warrington	Lost	15-22	14,462
Sat. 12 -	**GT. BRITAIN (2)**	**Lost**	**12-27**	**24,443**
Wed. 16 -	Castleford	Won	31-7	2,440
Sat. 19 -	Rochdale H.	Won	17-16	9,300
Wed. 23 -	Bradford N.	Won	11-6	5,271
Sat. 26 -	Salford	Won	21-5	4,000
December				
Sat. 3 -	Wakefield T.	Won	27-16	4,838
Wed. 7 -	N.R.L. X111	Lost	11-24	3,643
Sat. 10 -	Keighley	Drew	11-11	4,200
Sat. 17 -	**GT. BRITAIN (3)**	**Won**	**28-13**	**10,438**

Challenge Cup Finals

The famous Twin Towers of Wembley provided a magnificent backdrop to Rugby League Challenge Cup Finals, this picture from 1952 as Featherstone Rovers go on the attack against Workington Town.

THE RUGBY LEAGUE CHALLENGE CUP COMPETITION
FINAL TIE
FEATHERSTONE ROVERS v WORKINGTON TOWN
SATURDAY, APRIL 19th, 1952 KICK-OFF

The Empire Stadium
WEMBLEY

(Above) The 1952 Cup Final brought two new names to Wembley, and it was Workington Town who triumphed over Featherstone Rovers to win the trophy.

The Challenge Cup was the blue riband event of Rugby League, with an appearance underneath the Twin Towers of Wembley Stadium the dream of every club. Epic battles were fought in the earlier rounds of the Cup in front of big crowds, all with the dream of being able to walk out into the sunshine on that springtime Saturday afternoon at Wembley. During the 1950s, eleven different clubs appeared at Wembley, and there were seven different winners of the Challenge Cup in ten years. Wigan, Barrow and Workington Town all played in three Wembley Finals, Wigan winning all three whilst the two north-west teams could only manage one victory apiece.

After Australian Harry Bath had captained Warrington to their victory in 1950, the following year Cec Mountford became the first New Zealander to captain a Challenge Cup winning team at Wembley. Gus Risman, who had skippered Salford before the war, became the oldest player (at the age of 41) to lead a Cup winning side at Wembley when he guided the young Workington club to victory over Featherstone Rovers in 1952 after one of the most entertaining Finals the Empire Stadium had seen. Two years later it was a much more dour affair as Warrington and Halifax fought out the first drawn Wembley Final, resulting in a replay at Bradford's Odsal Stadium which was to produce a world record crowd and a place in sporting folklore.

(*Above*) Action from the 1953 Challenge Cup Final as Huddersfield's former All Black international wing, Peter Henderson faces his St.Helens opponent Stan McCormick, on the way to Fartown's 15-10 victory. (*Right*) Brian Bevan and Tommy Sale meet in the 1950 Wembley Final between Warrington and Widnes, which the Wire won 19-nil.

Challenge Cup Finals in the 'Fifties

1950

Saturday 6th May 1950, at Wembley Stadium
Warrington 19, Widnes 0
Warrington: Tries: Ryder, Knowelden, Bath.
Goals: Palin (5).
WARRINGTON: L.Jones; B.Bevan, R.Ryder, A.Naughton, A.Johnson; B.Knowelden, G.Helme; W.Derbyshire, H.Fishwick, R.Fisher, H.Bath, G.Lowe, H.Bath.
WIDNES: F.Bradley; J.Parkes, C.Hutton, T.Sale, A.Malone; J.Fleming, H.Anderson; R.Rowbottom, R.Band, C.Wilcox, F.Leigh, J.Naughton, C.Reynolds.
Referee: Mr. A. S. Dobson (Pontefract)
Attendance: 94,249. Receipts: £24,782.

1951

Saturday 5th May 1951, at Wembley Stadium.
Wigan 10, Barrow 0.
Wigan: Tries: Hilton, Gee.
Goals: Mountford, Gee.
WIGAN: J.Cunliffe; J.Hilton, J.Broome, G.Roughley, B.Nordgren; C.Mountford, T.Bradshaw; K.Gee, G.Curran, F.Barton, N.Silcock, T.Slevin, W.Blan.

1950 - Harry Bath leads Warrington.

BARROW: H.Stretch; J.Lewthwaite, P.Jackson, D.Goodwin, F.Castle; W.Horne, T.Toohey; F.Longman, J.McKinnell, R.Hartley, J.Grundy, H.Atkinson, H.McGregor.
Referee: Mr. M. Coates (Pudsey)
Attendance: 94,262. Receipts: £24,797.

1952

Saturday 19th April 1952, at Wembley Stadium.
Workington Town 18, Featherstone R. 10.
Workington Town: Tries: Lawrenson (2), Wilson, Mudge. Goals: Risman (3).
Featherstone: Tries: Batten, Evans. Goals: Miller (2).
WORKINGTON TOWN: A.J.Risman; J.Lawrenson, A.Paskins, E.Gibson, G.Wilson; J.Thomas, A.Pepperell; J.Hayton, V.McKeating, J.Wareing, J.Mudge, B.Wilson, W.Ivison.
FEATHERSTONE R.: F.Miller; E.Batten, D.Metcalfe, A.Tennant, N.Mitchell; R.Cording, R.Evans; K.Welburn, W.Bradshaw, J.Daly, F.Hulme, L.Gant, C.Lambert.
Referee: Mr. C. F. Appleton (Warrington)
Attendance: 72,093. Receipts: £22,374.

1953

Saturday 25th April 1953, at Wembley Stadium.
Huddersfield 15, St.Helens 10.
Huddersfield: Tries: Ramsden (2), Banks.
Goals: Cooper (2), Devery.
St.Helens: Tries: Llewellyn, Langfield. Goals: Langfield (2).
HUDDERSFIELD: J.Hunter; P.Henderson, R.Pepperell, P.Devery, L.Cooper; P.Ramsden, W.Banks; T.Slevin, G.Curran, J.Bowden, J.Brown, J.Large, D.Valentine.
ST.HELENS: G.Moses; S.Llewellyn, D.Geenall, D.Gullick, S.McCormick; J.Honey, G.Langfield; A.Prescott, R.Blakemore, G.Parr, G.Parsons, W.Bretherton, R.Cale.
Referee: Mr. G. S. Phillips (Widnes)
Attendance: 89,588. Receipts: £30,865.

The joy of winning the Cup at Wembley.

(Left) Barrow were Challenge Cup winners for the first time in 1955 and here they raise their inspirational leader Willie Horne aloft with the trophy. Barrow were back at Wembley two years later, but this time could not prevent Leeds from winning the Cup - narrowly by two points - which (above) allowed the very happy Loiners to celebrate as they chair their captain Keith McLellan.

1954

Saturday 24th April 1954, at Wembley Stadium.
Halifax 4, Warrington 4.
Halifax: Goals: Griffiths (2).
Warrington: Goals: Bath (2).
HALIFAX: T.Griffiths; A.Daniels, T.Lynch, P.Todd, D.Bevan; K.Dean, S.Kielty; J.Thorley, A.Ackerley, J.Wilkinson, A.Fearnley, S.Schofield, D.Clarkson.
WARRINGTON: E.Frodsham; B.Bevan, J.Challinor, A.Stevens, S.McCormick; R.Price, G.Helme; D.Naughton, F.Wright, G.Lowe, H.Bath, A.Heathwood, R.Ryan.
Referee: Mr. R. Gelder (Wakefield).
Attendance: 81,777. Receipts: £29,706.

1954 - Replay

Wednesday 5th May 1954, at Odsal Stadium, Bradford.
Warrington 8, Halifax 4.
Warrington: Tries: Challinor, Helme. Goal: Bath.
Halifax: Goals: Griffiths (2).
WARRINGTON: E.Frodsham; B.Bevan, J.Challinor, R.Ryder, S.McCormick; R.Price, G.Helme; D.Naughton, F.Wright, G.Lowe, H.Bath, A.Heathwood, R.Ryan.
HALIFAX: T.Griffiths; A.Daniels, T.Lynch, W.Mather, D.Bevan; K.Dean, S.Kielty; J.Thorley, A.Ackerley, J.Wilkinson, A.Fearnley, D.Schofield, D.Clarkson.
Referee: Mr. R. Gelder (Wakefield).
Attendance: 102,569. Receipts: £18,623.

1955

Saturday 30th April 1955, at Wembley Stadium.
Barrow 21, Workington Town 12.
Barrow: Tries: Goodwin, Castle, McKeating.
Goals: Horne (6).
Workington: Tries: Gibson, Faulder. Goals: Paskins (3).
BARROW: C.Best; J.Lewthwaite, P.Jackson, D.Goodwin, F.Castle; W.Horne, T.Toohey; L.Belshaw, V. McKeating, F.Barton, J.Grundy, R.Parker, W.Healey.
WORKINGTON TOWN: J.Vickers; I.Southward, A.Paskins, E.Gibson, E.Faulder; W.Wookey, J.Roper; J.Hayton, W.Lymer, A.Key, J.Mudge, B.Edgar, W.Ivison.
Referee: Mr. R. Gelder (Wakefield).
Attendance: 66,513. Receipts: £27,453.

1956

Saturday 28th April 1956, at Wembley Stadium
St.Helens 13, Halifax 2.
St.Helens: Tries: Carlton, Llewellyn, Prescott.
Goals: Rhodes (2).
Halifax: Goal: Griffiths.
ST.HELENS: G.Moses; S.Llewellyn, D.Greenall, B.Howard, F.Carlton; W.Finnan, A.Rhodes; A.Prescott, L.McIntyre, D.Silcock, G.Parsons, R.Robinson, V.Karalius.
HALIFAX: T.Griffiths; A.Daniels, T.Lynch, G.Palmer, J.Freeman; K.Dean, S.Kielty; J.Wilkinson, A.Ackerley, J.Henderson, L.Pearce, A.Fearnley, K.Traill.
Referee: Mr. R. Gelder (Wakefield).
Attendance: 79,341. Receipts: £29,424.

Wigan enjoyed two successive Wembley triumphs at the end of the 'fifties - the first, in 1958 over Workington Town, was very close and controversial as the Cumbrians were the victims of some debatable decisions - not least when stand-off Harry Archer was knocked out by a high tackle by winger Mick Sullivan *(pictured, left.)* Things were much better the following year when Wigan produced sparkling rugby to beat Hull, one of their six tries being scored by Brian McTigue *(above)* with John Barton and Roy Evans in support.

1957

Saturday 11th May 1957, at Wembley Stadium
Leeds 9, Barrow 7.
Leeds: Tries: Quinn, Hodgkinson, Robinson.
Barrow: Try: Jackson. Goals: Horne (2).
LEEDS: .P.Quinn; D.Hodgkinson, K.McLellan, L.Jones, G.Broughton; J.Lendill, J.Stevenson; J.Anderson, B.Prior, W.Hopper, B.Poole, D.Robinson, H.Street.
BARROW: J.Ball; J.Lewthwaite, P.Jackson, J.Rea, F.Castle; W.Horne, J.Harris; G.Woosey, M.Redhead, R.Parker, J.Grundy, D.Wilson, W.Healey.
Referee: Mr. C. F. Appleton (Warrington).
Attendance: 76,318. Receipts: £32,617

(Above) The 1957 Cup Final as Barrow's Reg Parker and Phil Jackson produce a vital tackle to prevent Leeds crossing their line at Wembley.

1958

Saturday 10th May 1958, at Wembley Stadium.
Wigan 13, Workington Town 9.
Wigan: Tries: Sullivan, Barton, McTigue.
Goals: Cunliffe (2).
Workington: Try: Southward. Goals: Southward (3).
WIGAN: J.Cunliffe; T.O'Grady, E.Ashton, W.Boston, M.Sullivan; D.Bolton, R.Thomas; J.Barton, W.Sayer, B.McTigue, N.Cherrington, F.Collier, B.McGurrin.
WORKINGTON: J.McAvoy; I.Southward, J.O'Neill, D.Leatherbarrow, W.Wookey; H.Archer, J.Roper; N.Herbert, H.Eden, A.Key, B.Edgar, C.Thompson, B.Eve.
Referee: Mr. R. Gelder (Wakefield).
Attendance: 66,109. Receipts: £33,175.

1959

Saturday 9th May 1959, at Wembley Stadium.
Wigan 30, Hull 13.
Wigan: Tries: Boston (2), Holden, Sullivan, Bolton, Mc.Tigue. Goals: Griffiths (6).
Hull: Try: Finn. Goals: Keegan (5).
WIGAN: F.Griffiths; W.Boston, E.Ashton, K.Holden, M.Sullivan; D.Bolton, R.Thomas; W.Bretherton, W.Sayer, J.Barton, N.Cherrington, B.McTigue, R.Evans.
HULL: A.Keegan; S.Cowan, B.Cooper, B.Saville, I.Watts; G.Matthews, T.Finn; M.Scott, T.Harris, J.Drake, C.Sykes, W.Drake, J.Whiteley.
Referee: Mr. C. F. Appleton (Warrington).
Attendance: 79,811. Receipts: 35,718.

Championship Finals

(Right)
Emergency winger Nat Silcock leaves Huddersfield's star Australian trio of Lionel Cooper, Pat Devery and Johnny Hunter in his wake as he dives over to score Wigan's opening try in their famous 1950 Championship Final victory at Maine Road, Manchester.

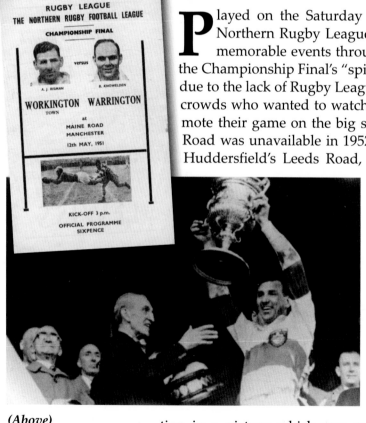

RUGBY LEAGUE
THE NORTHERN RUGBY FOOTBALL LEAGUE

CHAMPIONSHIP FINAL

A. J. RISMAN versus R. KNOWELDEN

WORKINGTON   WARRINGTON
TOWN

at
MAINE ROAD
MANCHESTER

12th MAY, 1951

KICK-OFF 3 p.m.

OFFICIAL PROGRAMME
SIXPENCE

(Above)
Gus Risman, player-coach of Workington Town, receives the Championship trophy in 1951 from Mr. Bob Anderton, whose Warrington side had just been defeated.

Played on the Saturday following the Cup Final at Wembley, the Northern Rugby League Championship Final produced a series of memorable events throughout the 'fifties. The decade opened with the Championship Final's "spiritual home" located at Maine Road - partly due to the lack of Rugby League grounds big enough to accommodate the crowds who wanted to watch them, and also the League's desire to promote their game on the big stage in the north's major city. When Maine Road was unavailable in 1952, the game broke new ground by going to Huddersfield's Leeds Road, before turning to the vast Odsal bowl at Bradford in 1957 and thereafter.

The first Championship Final of the 'fifties produced a sensational story as Wigan, without eight of their top players on their way to Australia with the 1950 Great Britain touring team, outplayed the star-studded Huddersfield team. Wigan's eight "A" teamers played the game of their lives, under the leadership of Cec Mountford, to win 20-2. A masterstroke by Wigan coach Jim Sullivan had been to play forward Nat Silcock on the wing to counter the threat of Huddersfield's block-buster Lionel Cooper. The plan worked to perfection in a victory which was regarded as the Wigan club's greatest ever achievement. Another plan came good the following year as the veteran Gus Risman captained his Workington Town team to a win over Warrington - when he was first appointed as manager-coach to the new Cumbrian club, Gus announced he had a 'seven year plan' to bring a major trophy to Workington, and by claiming the Championship title in 1951 in only their sixth season of existence, Town were ahead of schedule. It was a remarkable achievement for Risman, whose team took a huge following to Maine Road.

Wigan claimed their second Championship title of the decade when they beat Bradford Northern in the 1952 Final, played at the Huddersfield Town football ground, Leeds Road. Bradford had finished top of the league with Wigan second, but it was the Lancashire side who prevailed in the decider in front of over 48,000. Utility back Jack Cunliffe - playing at stand-off - was Wigan's captain *(pictured, above)* and it was his try which put Wigan in front.

(Above)
St.Helens captain Doug Greenall lifts the Championship trophy at Maine Road in 1953.

Championship Finals in the 'Fifties

1950

Saturday 13th May 1950, at Maine Road, Manchester
Wigan 20, Huddersfield 2.
Wigan: Tries: *Silcock, Broome, Nordgren, Blan.*
Goals: *Ward (4).*
Huddersfield: Goal: *Bawden.*
WIGAN: E.Ward; N.Silcock; J.Broome, G.Roughley; B.Nordgren; C.Mountford, J.Alty; E.Slevin, H.McIntyre, F.Barton, W.Hudon, J.Large, W.Blan.
HUDDERSFIELD: J.Hunter; R.Cracknell, J.Bawden, P.Devery, L.Cooper; R.Pepperell, W.Banks; J.Daly, J.Mundy, A.Wilmot, K.Morrison, R.Nicholson, I.Owens.
Referee: *Mr. M. Coates (Pudsey.)*
Attendance: *65,065.* **Receipts:** *£11,500.*

1951

Saturday 12th May 1951, at Maine Road, Manchester.
Workington Town 26, Warrington 11.
Workington: Tries: *Gibson (2), Wilson (2), Lawrenson, Paskins.* **Goals:** *Risman (4).*
Warrington: Tries: *Heathwood (2), Jackson.* **Goal:** *Bath.*
WORKINGTON: A.J.Risman; J.Lawrenson, A.Paskins, E.Gibson, G.Wilson; J.Thomas, A.Pepperell; J.Hayton, V.McKeating, J.Wareing, J.Mudge, S.Thurlow, W.Ivison.
WARRINGTON: E.Frodsham; B.Bevan, W.Jackson, A.Naughton, A.Johnson; B.Knowelden, G.Helme; W.Derbyshire, H.Fishwick, J.Atherton, H.Bath, R.Ryan, A.Heathwood.
Referee: *Mr. A. Hill (Dewsbury.)*
Attendance: *61,618.* **Receipts:** *£10,993.*

1952

Saturday 10th May 1952, at Leeds Road, Huddersfield.
Wigan 13, Bradford Northern 6.
Wigan: Tries: *Ryan, Cunliffe, Silcock.* **Goals:** *Gee (2).*
Bradford: Goals: *Phillips (3).*
WIGAN: M.Ryan; J.Hilton, J.Broome, G.Roughley, B.Nordgren; J.Cunliffe, J.Alty; K.Gee, R.Mather, G.Woosey, N.Silcock, J.Large, H.Street.
BRADFORD: J.Phillips; R.Hawes, J.Mageen, N.Hastings, G.McLean; L.Haley, G.Jones; W.Shreeve, N.Haley, B.Radford, B.Tyler, T.Foster, K.Traill.
Referee: *Mr. C. F. Appleton (Warrington.)*
Attendance: *48,684.* **Receipts:** *£8,215.*

1953

Saturday 9th May 1953, at Mainse Road, Manchester.
St.Helens 24, Halifax 14.
St.Helens: Tries: *Blakemore (2), Moses, Greenall, Cale, Metcalfe.* **Goals:** *Metcalfe (3).*
Halifax: Tries: *Lynch, Wilkinson.* **Goals:** *Griffiths (4).*
ST.HELENS: G.Moses; S.Llewellyn, D.Greenall, D.Gullick, S.McCormick; P.Metcalfe, J.Dickinson; A.Prescott, R.Blakemore, G.Parr, G.Parsons, W.Bretherton, R.Cale.
HALIFAX: T.Griffiths; B.Vierod, T.Lynch, M.Creeney, T.Cook; K.Dean, S.Kielty; M.Condon, A.Ackerley, J.Wilkinson, A.Fearnley, H.Greenwood, D.Clarkson.
Referee: *Mr. A. Hill (Dewsbury.)*
Attendance: *51,083.* **Receipts:** *£11,500.*

(Above)
Gerry Helme with the Championship trophy in 1954 after his Warrington team had completed the cup and league 'double.' The Wire beat Halifax in both Finals, with scrum-half Helme a key influence. Warrington retained the Championship in 1955.

Hull played in three consecutive Championship Finals in the 'fifties, winning two. Their first success came in 1956 when they beat luckless Halifax 10-9 at Manchester's Maine Road - the winning points coming with a penalty goal by Hull full-back Colin Hutton in the dying seconds of the match, leading to skipper Mick Scott raising the trophy *(above.)*

1954

Saturday 8th May 1954, at Maine Road, Manchester.
Warrington 8, Halifax 7.
Warrington: Goals: Bath (4).
Halifax: Try: Thorley. Goals: Griffiths (2).
WARRINGTON:. E.Frodsham; B.Bevan, J.Challinor, R.Ryder, S.McCormick; R.Price, G.Helme; D.Naughton, F.Wright, G.Lowe, H.Bath, A.Heathwood, R.Ryan.
HALIFAX: T.Griffiths; A.Daniels, T.Lynch, P.Todd, D.Bevan; K.Dean, S.Kielty; J.Thorley, A.Ackerley, J.Wilkinson, D.Schofield, A.Fearnley, D.Clarkson.
Referee: Mr. A. Hill (Dewsbury.)
Attendance: 36,519. Receipts: £9,076.

1955

Saturday 14th May 1955, at Maine Road, Manchester.
Warrington 7, Oldham 3.
Warrington: Try: Bevan. Goals: Bath (2).
Oldham: Try: Pitchford.
WARRINGTON: E.Frodsham; B.Bevan, J.Challinor, A.Naughton, L.Horton; J.Honey, G.Helme; D.Naughton, T.McKinney, G.Lowe, S.Phillips, H.Bath, R.Ryan.
OLDHAM: F.Stirrup; R.Barrow, R.Cracknell, A.Davies, T.O'Grady; F.Daley, F.Pitchford; H.Ogden, J.Keith, K.Jackson, C.Winslade, S.Little, B.Goldswain.
Referee: Mr. A. Hill (Dewsbury.)
Attendance: 49,434. Receipts: £11,516.

1956

Saturday 12th May 1956, at Maine Road, Manchester.
Hull 10, Halifax 9.
Hull: Tries: Finn, Harris. Goals: Hutton (2).
Halifax: Tries: Daniels, Palmer, Freeman.
HULL: C.Hutton; B.Darlington, B.Cooper, J.Watkinson, K.Bowman; C.Turner, T.Finn; M.Scott, T.Harris, R.Coverdale, H.Markham, W.Drake, J.Whiteley.
HALIFAX: P.Briers; A.Daniels, T.Lynch, G.Palmer, J.Freeman; K.Dean, S.Kielty; J.Thorley, A.Ackerley, J.Wilkinson, J.Henderson, D.Schofield, K.Traill.
Referee: Mr. C. F. Appleton (Warrington.)
Attendance: 36,675. Receipts: £9,179.

1957

Saturday 18th May 1957, at Odsal Stadium, Bradford.
Oldham 15, Hull 14.
Oldham: Tries: Etty (2), Ayres.
Goals: Ganley (3).
Hull: Tries: Cowan, Turner. Goals: Hutton (4).
OLDHAM: B.Ganley; R.Cracknell, A.Davies, D.Ayres, J.Etty; F.Daley, F.Pitchford; K.Jackson, J.Keith, D.Vines, S.Little, C.Winslade, D.Turner.
HULL: C.Hutton; S.Cowan, G.Dannatt, C.Turner, I.Watts; R.Moat, T.Finn; M.Scott, T.Harris, J.Drake, C.Sykes, W.Drake, J.Whiteley.
Referee: Mr. M. Coates (Pudsey.)
Attendance: 62,233. Receipts: £12,054.

(Above) The moment of glory finally came for Oldham's great side when they won their first Championship title in 1957, beating Hull by just a single point in front of over 62,000 at Odsal. The picture shows Oldham's scrum-half Frank Pitchford and second-rower Charlie Winslade put the squeeze on Hull's centre Dannatt in a thrilling match. Oldham were captained by full-back Bernard Ganley, and had two tries by winger John Etty as they took the trophy to Watersheddings.

Hull got revenge for their 1957 Final loss when they knocked Oldham out in the top-four semi-final the following year, and went on to become Champions from fourth place. They beat an injury-hit Workington side in the 1958 Final, enabling Johnny Whiteley to receive the trophy (above) from Lord Derby. The Championship of 1959 went to St.Helens in an orgy of points and spectacular play against Hunslet in scorching sunshine at Odsal. Saints winger Tom van Vollenhoven (right) scored a brilliant try hat-trick.

1958

Saturday 17th May 1958, at Odsal Stadium, Bradford.

Hull 20, Workington Town 3.

Hull: Tries: Cooper, Finn, Scott, J.Whiteley.
Goals: Bateson (4).
Workington: Try: Southward.
HULL: P.Bateson; I.Watts, B.Cooper, B.Saville, G.Dannatt; F.Broadhurst, T.Finn; M.Scott, T.Harris, B.Hambling, C.Sykes, P.Whiteley, J.Whiteley.
WORKINGTON: J.McAvoy; I.Southward, J.O'Neill, D.Leatherbarrow, K.Faulder; H.Archer, J.Roper; N.Herbert, H.Eden, T.Stamper, B.Edgar, C.Thompson, B.Eve.
Referee: Mr. R. Gelder (Wakefield.)
Attendance: 57,699. Receipts: £11,149.

1959

Saturday 16th May 1959, at Odsal Stadium, Bradford.

St.Helens 44, Hunslet 22.

St.Helens: Tries: Van Vollenhoven (3), Murphy (2), Prinsloo, Smith, Huddart. **Goals:** Rhodes (10).
Hunslet: Tries: Stockdill, Doyle, Poole, Gunney.
Goals: Langton (5).
ST.HELENS: A.Rhodes; T.Van Vollenhoven, D.Greenall, B.McGinn, J.Prinsloo; W.Smith, A.Murphy, A.Terry, T.McKinney, A.Prescott, B.Briggs, R.Huddart, V.Karalius.
HUNSLET: W.Langton; R.Colin, J.Stockdill, A.Preece, W.Walker; B.Gabbitas, K.Doyle; D.Hatfield, S. Smith, K.Eyre, H.Poole, G.Gunney, B.Shaw.
Referee: Mr. G. Wilson (Dewsbury.)
Attendance: 52,560. Receipts: £10,146.

Lancashire Cup Finals

(Above)
A happy Oldham team, with Dick Cracknell and Bernard Ganley holding the trophy, celebrate their third successive Lancashire Cup Final win in 1958.

(Above)
Leigh players show their joy at winning the Lancashire Cup in 1952, among them Rex Mossop, Trevor Allan and Joe Egan.

The 1950s was a glorious decade for the Lancashire Cup with a succession of big crowds drawn to a series of titanic Finals, all shared between Wigan's Central Park and Swinton's Station Road. Three crowds of over 40,000 were posted, and the Lancashire Cup Final attendance dipped below 30,000 on only two occasions, illustrating just how much Rugby League supporters loved the glamour of cup competitions.

Those Lancashire Cup Final crowds were considerably bigger than their Yorkshire Cup equivalents, a sign that the game's glamour clubs then were west of the Pennines - in the shape of Wigan, Warrington, St.Helens and Oldham. Another club who were determined to break into that exclusive group of trophy-winning outfits was Leigh, and they spent some huge amounts of money in trying to recruit a team that could bring glory to Kirkhall Lane.

Success came for Leigh in the shape of three Lancashire Cup Finals in the space of five years - two of them won. With full-back Jimmy Ledgard as safe as houses at the back, Leigh's big money signings included Wigan's international hooker Joe Egan and the Australian Rugby Union internationals Trevor Allan and Rex Mossop. They were all in the side which brought the Lancashire Cup back to Leigh in 1952, after a conclusive 22-5 win over St.Helens at Swinton; and Leigh repeated the dose in 1955 when they beat Widnes 26-9, this time at Central Park.

The decade began with two successive Lancashire Cups to Wigan. With 1950 tourists Joe Egan and Tommy Bradshaw both on their way out of Central Park (both eventually signing for Leigh) there were two Lancashire Cup winners' medals apiece for scrum-half Johnny Alty and hooker Ron Mather in the Wigan team. Meanwhile, St.Helens qualified for five Lancashire Cup Finals in the 'fifties, but won only one, in 1953.

Oldham became the dominant force with their much admired side which never got the Wembley Final they craved, but did win three consecutive Lancashire Cups in a trilogy of high drama in 1956, '57 and '58. A total of 120,821 spectators paid to see those three Finals as Oldham's brilliance saw off the challenges of St.Helens (twice) and Wigan.

The first of those three wins meant Oldham held the Lancashire Cup again for the first time in 23 years, and their victory over St.Helens at Wigan owed more to their mighty forward pack, including Don Vines, Syd Little, Charlie Winslade and Derek Turner, than to the usual Oldham flowing back play spearheaded by centre Alan Davies. It was a last minute try by Turner which sealed their 10-3 victory- bringing a winners' medal and £30 winning money.

(Right) Bernard Ganley, pictured whilst representing Great Britain, was a major figure for Oldham in their four Lancashire Cup Finals in the 1950s - three of them won.

(Above) Barrow's winger Derek Hinchley in the 1954 Lancashire Cup Final at Swinton, races Oldham's Terry O'Grady and Frank Pitchford to the ball.

Barrow got their hands on the Lancashire Cup for the first time in 1954, although it proved to be merely an appetizer for their exploits later in the same season when they went on to win the Challenge Cup at Wembley. Victory in the Lancashire Cup Final over Oldham brought great joy to the Furness area as Barrow, inevitably captained by the great Willie Horne, upset the pre-match tipsters. Barrow also surprised their own fans by selecting erstwhile second-rower Derek Hinchley on the right wing ahead of international Jimmy Lewthwaite, who was only travelling reserve that day at Station Road.

Lancashire Cup Finals in the 'Fifties

1950
Saturday 4th November 1950, at Station Road, Swinton.
Wigan 28, Warrington 5.
Wigan: Tries: Nordgren (2), Cunliffe, Roughley, Alty, Slevin. Goals: Gee (5).
Warrington: Try: Naughton. Goal: Palin.
WIGAN: J.Cunliffe; G.Ratcliffe, J.Broome, G.Roughley, B.Nordgren; C.Mountford, J.Alty; K.Gee, R.Mather, F.Barton, E.Slevin, N.Silcock, W.Blan.
WARRINGTON: E.Frodsham; B.Bevan, R.Ryder, A.Naughton, A.Johnson; B.Knowelden, G.Helme; W.Derbyshire, H.Fishwick, J.Featherstone, H.Bath, R.Ryan, H.Palin.
Referee: Mr. G. S. Phillips (Widnes.)
Attendance: 42,541. Receipts: £6,222.

1951
Saturday 27th October 1951, at Station Road, Swinton.
Wigan 14, Leigh 6.
Wigan: Tries: Nordgren (2), Broome, Large. Goal: Gee.
Leigh: Tries: Harris, Morgan.
WIGAN: J.Cunliffe; G.Ratcliffe, G.Roughley, E.Ashcroft, B.Nordgren; J.Broome, J.Alty; K.Gee, R.Mather, F.Barton, N.Silcock, J.Large, H.Street.
LEIGH: J.Ledgard; W.Kindon, T.Allan, N.Harris, F.Morgan; E.Kerwick, K.Baxter; H.Eddon, J.Egan, G.Burke, C.Pawsey, W.Tabern, P.Foster.
Referee: Mr. A. S. Dobson (Pontefract.)
Attendance: 33,230. Receipts: £5,432.

1952
Saturday 29th November 1952, at Station Road, Swinton.
Leigh 22, St.Helens 5.
Leigh: Tries: Kitchen (2), Chadwick, Allan.
Goals: Ledgard (5).
St.Helens: Try: Gullick. Goal: Langfield.
LEIGH: J.Ledgard; B.Chadwick, T.Allan, E.Kerwick, F.Kitchen; K.Baxter, T.Bradshaw; H.Eddon, J.Egan, S.Owen, C.Pawsey, R.Mossop, P.Foster.
ST.HELENS: J.Lowe; S.Llewellyn, D.Greenall, D.Gullick, S.McCormick; J.Honey, G.Langfield; A.Prescott, R.Blakemore, W.Whittaker, G.Parsons, W.Bretherton, R.Cale.
Referee: Mr. A. Hill (Dewsbury.)
Attendance: 34,785. Receipts: £5,793.

1953
Saturday 24th October 1953, at Station Road, Swinton.
St.Helens 16, Wigan 8.
St.Helens: Tries: Moses, Honey.
Goals: Metcalfe (5).
Wigan: Tries: Fleming, Street. Goal: Gee.
ST.HELENS: G.Moses; S.Llewellyn, D.Geenall, D.Gullick, S.McCormick; P.Metcalfe, J.Honey; A.Prescott, R.Blakemore, G.Parr, G.Parsons, W.Bretherton, V.Karalius.
WIGAN: J.Cunliffe; B.Nordgren, J.Broome, E.Ashcroft, R.Hurst; J.Fleming, J.Alty; K.Gee, R.Mather, N.Silcock, F.Collier, T.Horrocks, H.Street.
Referee: Mr. M. Coates (Pudsey.)
Attendance: 42,793. Receipts: £6,790.

Oldham's Yorkshiremen winners of Lancashire Cup

A feature of Oldham's Lancashire Cup winning sides of the 'fifties was the presence of numerous Yorkshiremen in the 'Roughyeds' team. None was more dominant than Derek "Rocky" Turner at loose-forward, pictured *(above, left)* putting pressure on St.Helens' scrum-half Alex Murphy in the 1958 Final at Station Road. *(Above, right)* "Yorkies" John Etty and Jack Keith proudly display the Lancashire Cup back at Watersheddings after Oldham's 1956 victory over St.Helens, whilst *(left)* is Dick Cracknell, who was a Yorkshire Cup winner with Huddersfield before winning the Lancashire Cup with Oldham.

1954

Saturday 23rd October 1954, at Station Road, Swinton.

Barrow 12, Oldham 2.

Barrow: Tries: Goodwin, Parker. Goals: Horne (3).
Oldham: Goal: Ganley.
BARROW: C.Poole; D.Hinchley, P.Jackson, D.Goodwin, F.Castle; W.Horne, T.Toohey; L.Belshaw, V.McKeating, F.Barton, J.Grundy, R.Parker, W.Healey.
OLDHAM: B.Ganley; R.Cracknell, R.Barrow, A.Davies, T.O'Grady; F.Daley, F.Pitchford; H.Ogden, J.Keith, K.Jackson, C.Winslade, S.Little, B.Goldswain.
Referee: Mr. R. Gelder (Wakefield.)
Attendance: 25,204. Receipts: £4,603.

1955

Saturday 15th October, at Central Park, Wigan.

Leigh 26, Widnes 9.

Leigh: Tries: Kindon, Gullick, Barton, Owen.
Goals: Ledgard (7).
Widnes: Try: Williamson. Goals: Sale (3).
LEIGH: J.Ledgard; W.Kindon, D.Gullick, A.Moore, M.Davies; J.Fleming, B.Chadwick; J.Barton, W.Tabern, S.Owen, D.Hurt, M.Martyn, P.Foster.
WIDNES: J.Sale; G.Williamson, H.Kinsey, H.Dawson, P.Ratcliffe; R.Butler, P.Davies; R.Rowbottom, J.Hayes, H.Tomlinson, V.Smith, G.Murray, G.Kemel.
Referee: Mr. R. Gelder (Wakefield.)
Attendance: 26,507. Receipts: £4,090.

1956

Saturday, 20th October 1956, at Central Park, Wigan.

Oldham 10, St.Helens 3.

Oldham: Tries: Etty, Turner. Goals: Ganley (2).
St.Helens: Try: Carlton.
OLDHAM: B.Ganley; R.Cracknell, D.Ayers, A.Davies, J.Etty; F.Stirrup, F.Pitchford; K.Jackson, J.Keith, D.Vines, S.Little, C.Winslade, D.Turner.
ST.HELENS: G.Moses; S.Llewellyn, D.Geenall, W.Finnan, F.Carlton; A.Rhodes, J.Dickinson; A.Prescott, L.McIntyre, D.Silcock, G.Parsons, J.Gaskell, V.Karalius.
Referee: Mr. M. Coates (Pudsey.)
Attendance: 39,544. Receipts: £6,274.

1957

Saturday 19th October 1957, at Station Road, Swinton.

Oldham 13, Wigan 8.

Oldham: Tries: Ganley, Davies, Pitchford.
Goals: Ganley (2).
Wigan: Tries: O'Grady, McTigue. Goal: Cunliffe.
OLDHAM: B.Ganley; R.Cracknell, V.Nestor, A.Davies, J.Etty; F.Daley, F.Pitchford; K.Jackson, J.Keith, D.Vines, C.Winslade, S.Little, D.Turner.
WIGAN: J.Cunliffe; R.Chisnall, E.Ashton, E.Ashcroft, T.O'Grady; W.Boston, D.Bolton; A.Armstrong, W.Sayer, B.McTigue, N.Cherrington, W.Bretherton, B.McGurrin.
Referee: Mr. M. Coates (Pudsey.)
Attendance: 42,497. Receipts: £6,918.

(Left)
The dramatic moment that turned the 1959 Final Warrington's way, as Brian Bevan stretches out ahead of Tom van Vollenhoven and was awarded a try.

(Below)
The captains, Alan Prescott of St.Helens and Eric Fraser of Warrington, lead their teams out at Central Park for the 1959 Lancashire Cup Final.

The final Lancashire Cup Final of the 'fifties proved to be one of the most dramatic, and certainly the most controversial, as Warrington and St.Helens fought out a nail-biting contest before almost 40,000 spectators at Wigan's Central Park. The "Wire" won by a single point, 5-4, after the game's only try was scored by the maestro Brian Bevan as he chased a kick ahead to get fingertips to the ball just before it crossed the dead-ball line. Many in the crowd thought Bevan had not got the touchdown, and St.Helens' South African flyer Tom van Vollenhoven was sure he had kicked the ball dead before Bevan got his hand on it - but only man who mattered was referee Matt Coates, and he said it was a try. Subsequently, the match-winner Bevan was carried shoulder high from the field by delighted Warrington fans as they celebrated a first Lancashire Cup winners' medal for the legendary Australian winger. Saints had been hot favourites to win the trophy, but fate decreed it would be Bevan's day.

1958
Saturday 25th October 1958, at Station Road, Swinton.
Oldham 12, St.Helens 2.
Oldham: Tries: Davies, Kellett.
Goals: Ganley (2), Kellett.
St.Helens: Goal: Fearis.
OLDHAM: B.Ganley; R.Cracknell, A.Davies, J.Noon, J.Etty; A.Kellett, F.Pitchford; R.Rowbottom, J.Keith, K.Jackson, C.Winslade, D.McKeown, D.Turner.
ST.HELENS: P.Fearis; T.Van Vollenhoven, D.Greenall, K.Large, F.Carlton; B.Howard, A.Murphy; A.Terry, T.McKinney, D.Brown, B.Briggs, W.Delves, V.Karalius.
Referee: Mr. R. Gelder (Wakefield.)
Attendance: 38,780. Receipts: £6,933.

1959
Saturday 31st October 1959, at Central Park, Wigan.
Warrington 5, St.Helens 4.
Warrington: Try: Bevan. Goal: Fraser.
St.Helens: Goals: Rhodes (2).
WARRINGTON: E.Fraser, B.Bevan, J.Challinor, L.Gilfedder, T.O'Grady; R.Greenhough, J.Edwards; N.Silcock, P.Lannon, A.Brindle, J.Arkwright, H.Major, A.Naughton.
ST.HELENS: A.Rhodes; T.Van Vollenhoven, D.Greenall, B.McGinn, J.Prinsloo; A.Murphy, W.Smith; A.Terry, T.McKinney, A.Prescott, B.Briggs, R.Huddart, F.Terry.
Referee: Mr. M. Coates (Pudsey.)
Attendance: 39,237. Receipts: £6,424.

Yorkshire Cup Finals

The Yorkshire Cup, as one of the coveted "All Four Cups" of Rugby League, was a major attraction for every club east of the Pennines, and throughout the 1950s provided the opportunity for players and supporters alike to enjoy the season's first taste of silverware and thrills of knockout football.

More than that, Yorkshire Cup Finals gave some of the less fashonable teams a real chance to enjoy their day in the sun, and it usually was that quite literally, as the Finals were staged in the late Autumn sunshine, most often at Headingley. Castleford, Keighley, Batley and York all took part in Yorkshire Cup Finals in the 'fifties, and it was a real feather in their caps to get there and take on the white-rose elite like Huddersfield, Leeds, Halifax, Hull and Wakefield.

The decade began with the claret and gold of Huddersfield still flying high as one of the game's most attractive and cosmopolitan teams, and they won two Yorkshire Cups, in 1950 and '52, helped coniderably by their Aussie stars Lionel Cooper, Pat Devery and Johnny Hunter in the back division - but on neither occasion did the men from Fartown find it easy against Castleford and Batley. Bradford Northern were another club who had enjoyed a golden era in the post-war years, and as times began to change at Odsal they managed one last major trophy before their great side finally broke up when they won the Yorkshire Cup in 1953.

(Above)
Huddersfield captain Lionel Cooper holds the Yorkshire Cup and Russell Pepperell the plinth, after their victory in the 1950 Final. Dick Cracknell and Billy Banks are also in the picture.

Getting to a Yorkshire Cup Final was a real rarity for Keighley, they had only done it once before (during World War Two) when they lined up against Wakefield at Fartown in 1951. Trinity had won through following a major shock victory over Leeds at Headingley in the semi-final, and they beat Keighley 17-3 to take the trophy. For Wakefield, it was a precurson of more successful times to come, and they were back for another two Yorkshire Cup Finals as the decade progressed - winning against Hunslet in 1956 and going down to Leeds in a 44-point thriller in 1958.

(Above)
The Castleford team presented to the chief guests before their 1950 Yorkshire Cup Final at Headingley.

Poor old Hull were left to rue their bad luck in the Yorkshire Cup as the 'fifties came to an end, after they played in no less than five Finals (including a replay against Halifax in 1955) and lost them all. International forwards Johnny Whiteley, Mick Scott and Tommy Harris were among the Hull men who played in all five of those Finals and finished as runners-up, as the famous Airlie Birds' pack were unable to take the Yorkshire Cup back to the Boulevard.

Batley had not appeared in a major Final for many years when they lined up against Huddersfield in 1952, and the "Gallant Youths" took the mighty claret and golds all the way before the Yorkshire Cup finally went to Fartown, in a season in which Huddersfield went on to win at Wembley.

Bradford Northern's Yorkshire Cup in 1953 proved to be a last "hurrah" of the great post-war era at Odsal. Fittingly, it was Trevor Foster (pictured, left) one of their finest stalwarts of that successful team, who captained Northern as they beat Hull 7-2.

(Above)
Batley winger John Etty dives over to score in the 1952 Final against Huddersfield, as the game ended in near darkness.

Yorkshire Cup Finals in the 'Fifties

1950
Saturday 4th November 1950, at Headingley, Leeds.
Huddersfield 16, Castleford 3.
Huddersfield: Tries: Pepperell (2). Goals: Bawden (5).
Castleford: Try: Lloyd.
HUDDERSFIELD: J.Hunter; R.Cracknell, J.Bawden, I.W.Clark, L.Cooper; R.Pepperell, W.Banks; F.Wagstaff, J.Mundy, A.Wilmot, R.Nicholson, I.Owens, D.Valentine.
CASTLEFORD: R.Lewis, L.Brown, P.Aldred, G.Broughton, R.Lloyd; A.Fisher, G.Langfield; J.Anderson, J.Jones, L.Fleming, C.Howard, L.Haughey, F.Mugglestone.
Referee: Mr. R. Gelder (Wakefield.)
Attendance: 28,906. Receipts: £5,152..

1951
Saturday 29th October 1951, at Fartown, Huddersfield.
Wakefield Trinity 17, Keighley 3.
Wakefield: Tries: Boocker, Robinson, Hughes.
Goals: Hirst (4).
Keighley: Try: Redman.
WAKEFIELD: E.Luckman; J.Duggan, L.Hirst, D.Froggatt, D.Boocker; G.Meredith, A.Fletcher; J.Booth, D.Horner, W.Hudson, W.J.D.Howes, D.Robinson, R.Hughes.
KEIGHLEY: G.Lockwood; L.Ward, F.Taylor, M.Creeney, W.Ivill; E.Redman, F.Barratt; C.Brereton, J.Britton, J.Ramsden, A.Mulhall, R.Kelly, Sanderson.
Referee: Mr. F. Smith (Barrow.)
Attendance: 25,495. Receipts: £3,347.

1952
Saturday 15th November 1952, at Headingley, Leeds.
Huddersfield 18, Batley 8.
Huddersfield: Tries: Cooper (3), Valentine.
Goals: Devery (3).
Batley: Tries: Kenny, Etty.
Goal: Laycock.
HUDDERSFIELD: J.Hunter; P.Henderson, P.Ramsden, P.Devery, L.Cooper; R.Pepperell, W.Banks; E.Slevin, G.Curran, W.Griffiths, J.Brown, J.Large, D.Valentine.
BATLEY: P.Walshaw; G.Harrison, G.Kenny, W.Riches, J.Etty; W.Riley, R.Laycock; H.Wagstaff, H.McIntyre, T.Jones, G.Palmer, C.Briggs, J.Westbury.
Referee: Mr. C. F. Appleton (Warrington.)
Attendance: 14,705. Receipts: 2,471.

1953
Saturday 31st October 1953, at Headingley, Leeds.
Bradford Northern 7, Hull 2.
Bradford: Try: Hawes.
Goals: Phillips (2).
Hull: Goal: Hutton.
BRADFORD: J.Phillips; R.Hawes, J.Mageen, W.Seddon, J.McLean; W.Jenkins, R.Goddard; B.Tyler, N.Haley, W.Jones, T.Foster, A.Storey, K.Traill.
HULL: C.Hutton; K.Bowman, W.Riches, C.Turner, I.Watts; B.Conway, A.Tripp; M.Scott, T.Harris, R.Coverdale, H.Markham, A.Bedford, J.Whiteley.
Referee: Mr. G. S. Phillips (Widnes.)
Attendance: 22,147. Receipts: £3,833.

(Above)
Halifax captain Alvin Ackerley led them to two Yorkshire Cup triumphs in 1954 and 1955. This Halifax side of the mid 'fifties is pictured *(right)* at Thrum Hall with coach "Dolly"Dawson on the left and star half-backs Dean and Kielty at the front.

Halifax's bad luck in finishing as runners-up in several Championship and Challenge Cup Finals in the 'fifties has been well documented, but they did find some consolation in the Yorkshire Cup in which they beat arch rivals Hull in consecutive Finals, in 1954 and '55 (the latter after a replay.) Skippered by the Cumbrian hooker Alvin Ackerley, Halifax had a mighty pack of forwards which included rugged characters like Albert Fearnley, Jack Wilkinson and Les Pearce, whose duels with the equally robust Hull set produced plenty of fire and brimstone before the Yorkshire Cup found its way to Thrum Hall.

1954

Saturday 29th October 1954, at Headingley, Leeds..
Halifax 22, Hull 14.
Halifax: Tries: Daniels (2), Ackerley, Pearce.
Goals: Griffiths (5).
Hull: Tries: Conway, Markham. Goals: Hutton (4).
HALIFAX: T.Griffiths; A.Daniels, T.Lynch, P.Todd, D.Bevan; K.Dean, S.Kielty; J.Thorley, A.Ackerley, L.Olsen, L.Pearce, J.Wilkinson, E.Callighan.
HULL: C.Hutton; K.Bowman, R.Francis, C.Turner, W.Riches; B.Conway, A.Tripp; M.Scott, T.Harris, R.Coverdale, H.Markham, N.Hockley, J.Whiteley.
Referee: Mr. T. W. Watkinson (Manchester.)
Attendance: 25,949. Receipts: £4,638.

1955

Saturday 22nd October 1955, at Headingley, Leeds.
Halifax 10, Hull 10.
Halifax: Tries: Bevan, Henderson. Goals: Griffiths (2).
Hull: Tries: Bowman, Watts. Goals: Watkinson (2).
HALIFAX: T.Griffiths; A.Daniels, T.Lynch, G.Palmer, D.Bevan; K.Dean, S.Kielty; J.Thorley, A.Ackerley, J.Wilkinson, D.Schofield, A.Fearnley.
HULL: J.Watkinson; K.Bowman, C.Turner, W.Riches, I.Watts; R.Moat, T.Finn; M.Scott, T.Harris, R.Coverdale, H.Markham, W.Drake, J.Whiteley.
Referee: Mr. G. S. Phillips (Widnes.)
Attendance: 23,520. Receipts: £4,385.

1955 - Replay

Wednesday 2nd November 1955, at Odsal Std', Bradford.
Halifax 7, Hull 0.
Halifax: Try: Daniels. Goals: Griffiths (2).
HALIFAX: T.Griffiths; A.Daniels, T.Lynch, G.Palmer, D.Bevan; K.Dean, S.Kielty; J.Thorley, A.Ackerley, J.Wilkinson, L.Pearce, D.Schofield, A.Fearnley.
HULL: C.Hutton; K.Bowman, W.Riches, C.Turner, I.Watts; R.Moat, T.Finn; M.Scott, T.Harris, R.Coverdale, H.Markham, W.Drake, J.Whiteley.
Referee: Mr. N. T. Railton (Wigan.)
Attendance: 14,000. Receipts: £2,315.

1956

Saturday 20th October 1956, at Headingley, Leeds.
Wakefield Trinity 23, Hunslet 5.
Wakefield: Tries: Smith (2), Cooper (2), A. Mortimer.
Goals: F. Mortimer (4).
Hunslet: Try: Child. Goal: Talbot.
WAKEFIELD: F.Mortimer; F.Smith, A.Mortimer, C.Bell, E.Cooper; K.Holliday, K.Rollin; D.Harrison, K.Bridges, F.Haigh, R.Kelly, P.Armstead, L.Chamberlain.
HUNSLET: W.Langton; F.Child, N.Stockdill, G.Waite, A.Preece; B.Gabbitas, A.Talbot; D.Hatfield, S.Smith, C.Cooper, B.Shaw, A.Clues, G.Gunney.
Referee: Mr. N. T. Railton (Wigan.)
Attendance: 31,147. Receipts: £5,607.

One of the attractions of the Yorkshire Cup was being able to see some of the game's so-called "smaller" clubs enjoy moments of glory, and so it was for York when they won through to the Final in 1957 and put up an admirable show before going down 15-8 to Huddersfield.

Even better was to follow for Featherstone Rovers in 1959. Already recognised as mighty cup fighters, the Rovers won the Yorkshire Cup for the first time in peacetime (they had won it previously in 1940 during the war) when they beat the much fancied Hull team at

Headingley. It was close, 15-14, but the Featherstone boys celebrated with great delight alongside their supporters as captain Joe Mullaney lifted the trophy. A key to their victory was hooker Willis Fawley's ability to supply possession by beating Hull's international star Tommy Harris in the scrums.

(Above)
Featherstone Rovers players and officials celebrate winning the Yorkshire Cup in 1959.

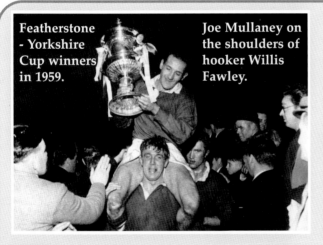

Featherstone - Yorkshire Cup winners in 1959.

Joe Mullaney on the shoulders of hooker Willis Fawley.

1957

Saturday 19th October 1957, at Headingley, Leeds.
Huddersfield 15, York 8.
Huddersfield: Tries: Kilroy, Smales, Bowman.
Goals: Dyson (3).
York: Tries: Flannery, Illingworth.. Goal: Yorke.
HUDDERSFIELD: F.Dyson; H.Plunkett, A.Kilroy, R.Barrow, M.Sullivan; P.Ramsden, T.Smales; E.Slevin, R.Wood, D.Flint, B.Briggs, K.Bowman, D.Valentine.
YORK: W.Hargreaves; B.Smith, D.Webster, G.Smith, S.Flannery; J.Robinson, W.Riley; F.Moore, R.Illingworth, V.Yorke, B.Watts, R.O'Brien, E.Dawson.
Referee: Mr. C. F. Appleton (Warrington.)
Attendance: 22,531. Receipts: £4,123.

1958

Saturday 18th October 1958, at Odsal Stadium, Bradford.
Leeds 24, Wakefield Trinity 20.
Leeds: Tries: Hemmingway (2), Quinn, Jones, Simms, Stevenson. Goals: Jones (3).
Wakefield: Tries: Metcalfe (3), Rollin.
Goals: F. Mortimer (2), Fox (2).
LEEDS: P.Quinn; G.Hemmingway, J.Lendill, L.Jones, D.Hodgkinson; G.Brown, J.Stevenson; A.Skelton, B.Simms, D.Robinson, C.Tomlinson, F.Ward, A.Dick.
WAKEFIELD: F.Mortimer; F.Smith, D.Metcalfe, N.Fox, S.Smith; K.Holliday, K.Rollin; W.Adams, J.Shaw, S.Evans, R.Kelly, L.Chamberlain, K.Traill.
Referee: Mr. C. F. Appleton (Warrington.)
Attendance: 26,927. Receipts: £3,830.

1959

Saturday 31st October 1959, at Headingley, Leeds.
Featherstone Rovers 15, Hull 14.
Featherstone: Tries: Woolford, Fox, Lambert.
Goals: Clawson (3).
Hull: Tries: Saville, Whiteley. Goals: Bateson (4).
FEATHERSTONE: J.Fennell; F.Smith, K.Greatorex; J.Hunt, C.Woolford; J.Mullaney, D.Fox; J.Anderson, W.Fawley, M.Dixon, M.Clamp, C.Lambert, T.Clawson.
HULL: P.Bateson; S.Cowan, B.Cooper, B.Saville, D.Nicholson; G.Matthews, T.Finn; M.Scott, T.Harris, J.Drake, C.Sykes, W.Drake, J.Whiteley.
Referee: Mr. C. F. Appleton (Warrington.)
Attendance: 23,983. Receipts: £4,156.

The County Championship

(Below) **Dick Huddart strides over to score one of his two tries for Cumberland in their 29-7 win over Yorkshire in 1958, with Leigh's Derek Hurt in support. It was Huddart's first game after returning from the successful 1958 Lions tour.**

(Above) **Centre Alan Davies on the way to one of his two tries for Lancashire in their 1956 'Roses' thrashing of Yorkshire at the Boulevard, Hull. Davies had just been served a pass by Norman Cherrington, as Ken Traill and Don Fox cover for Yorkshire.**

The County Championship during the 1950s saw honours evenly shared between Lancashire and Yorkshire, with each winning four titles. For Cumberland it was not a vintage decade, but as they won the final Championship of the 'fifties there were signs of the successes that were to follow in the 1960s. The County games were looked upon as excellent guidelines for the international selectors, but for the players it was always a source of pride to win their County cap.

With fixtures staged in midweek, it wasn't easy to guarantee player availability, but the County Championship was still a great attraction for the fans. The arrival of floodlights at Leigh added a new dimension for Lancashire as Hilton Park became a favourite home ground for them, drawing some excellent crowds. And Yorkshire got in on the act as Cumberland agreed to travel to Hull on a Monday night for their 1953 fixture under lights at Boothferry Park, an 11,787 attendance boosting the Yorkshire coffers.

(Above) **In Yorkshire's first home game of the 'Fifties, this was the white rose team at Fartown before beating Lancashire 23-15 on 18th October, 1950. Left to right:** (Standing): **Arthur Wilmot (Huddersfield), Bernard Poole (Leeds), Bill Metcalfe (Hunslet), Jim Bowden (Huddersfield), Jack Booth (Wakefield Trinity), John Etty (Batley), Ken Traill (Bradford.** (In front): **Alf Burnell (Hunslet), Arthur Wood (Featherstone), Dick Cracknell (Huddersfield), Ernest Ward (Bradford) captain, Ken Dean (Halifax) and Stan Thompson (Dewsbury).**

(*Above*) The Cumberland team before their 29-7 win over Yorkshire at Whitehaven on 15th September, 1958. Left to right: (*Standing*): Dick Huddart (Whitehaven), John O'Neill (Workington), Alvin Ackerley (Halifax), Derek Hurt (Leigh), Ted Stephenson (Workington), Billy Garratt (Whitehaven), Ray Donaldson (Barrow), Bill McAlone (Whitehaven). (*In front*): Ivor Watts (Hull), Louis Shepherd (Whitehaven), Syd Lowden (Salford), John 'Sol' Roper (Workington) and Ike Southward (Workington).

County Championships in the 'Fifties

1950-51
Cumberland 10, Yorkshire 5. (*at Whitehaven*)
Yorkshire 23, Lancashire 15. (*at Huddersfield*)
Lancashire 13, Cumberland 12. (*at Barrow*)
Champions: CUMBERLAND

1951-52
Yorkshire 25, Cumberland 3. (*at Hull K.R.*)
Lancashire 5, Yorkshire 15. (*at Leigh*)
Cumberland 11, Lancashire 19. (*at Whitehaven*)
Champions: YORKSHIRE

1952-53
Cumberland 8, Yorkshire 7. (*at Workington*)
Lancashire 41, Cumberland 14. (*at St.Helens*)
Yorkshire 16, Lancashire 8. (*at Hull*)
Champions: LANCASHIRE

1953-54
Cumberland 15, Lancashire 5. (*at Whitehaven*)
Yorkshire 16, Cumberland 7. (*at Boothferry Park,Hull*)
Lancashire 18, Yorkshire 10. (*at Leigh*).
Play-off: Cumberland 5, Yorkshire 9. (*at Whitehaven*)
Champions: YORKSHIRE

1954-55
Cumberland 0, Yorkshire 27. (*at Workington*)
Lancashire 24, Cumberland 7. (*at Wigan*)
Yorkshire 20, Lancashire 10. (*at Bradford*)
Champions: YORKSHIRE

1955-56
Cumberland 18, Lancashire 20. (*at Workington*)
Lancashire 26, Yorkshire 10. (*at Oldham*)
Yorkshire 14, Cumberland 2. (*at Bradford*)
Champions: LANCASHIRE

1956-57
Lancashire 42, Cumberland 21. (*at Wigan*)
Cumberland 15, Yorkshire 14. (*at Whitehaven*)
Yorkshire 21, Lancashire 35. (*at Hull*)
Champions: LANCASHIRE

1957-58
Yorkshire 27, Cumberland 18. (*at Hull*)
Cumberland 22, Lancashire 12. (*at Workington*)
Lancashire 11, Yorkshire 25. (*at Widnes*)
Champions: YORKSHIRE

1958-59
Lancashire 60, Cumberland 12. (*at Wigan*)
Cumberland 29, Yorkshire 7. (*at Whitehaven*)
Yorkshire 35, Lancashire 19. (*at Hull K.R.*)
Champions: LANCASHIRE

1959-60
Cumberland 14, Lancashire 8. (*at Workington*)
Yorkshire 13, Cumberland 26. (*at Hull*)
Lancashire 28, Yorkshire 38. (*at Leigh*)
Champions: CUMBERLAND
Total titles: Lancs. (4), Yorks (4), Cumberland (2).

The game in Australia

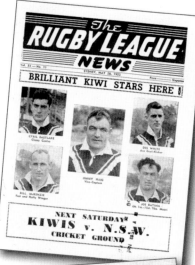

(*Above*)
How Australia welcomed overseas touring teams in a prolific decade for international League.

It was a wonderfully colourful and prolific decade for international Rugby League in Australia, with every single season of the 1950s lit up by the visit of a touring team. As well as the arrival of France as an exotic addition to the regular tour cycle and Test series with the long established rivals from Great Britain and New Zealand, the Aussies also played host to the American Allstars in 1953 and staged the World Cup in 1957. No individual dominated the Australian game more than Clive Churchill throughout the 'fifties, a decade which began in 1950 with him becoming the first Australian captain in 30 years to lift the Ashes trophy - a feat he managed to repeat in 1954.

Churchill, known by all in Australia as *The Little Master*, went on to make three Kangaroo tours as a player, captaining the 1952 side. He also came to Europe as captain of Australia's 1954 World Cup team, and by the end of the decade returned for a fourth Kangaroo tour as (non playing) coach of the 1959 team. In club football he was the lynchpin of the brilliant South Sydney team as they won five Premiership titles between 1950 and 1955. Churchill actually missed out on Souths' Grand Final win in 1955, after breaking his arm in their penultimate regular season match against Manly. That did not stop him booting the winning goal from the touchline that day at Redfern Oval after the full-time bell had sounded,

(*Above*) **Clive Churchill, playing rep. football for Brisbane in the Bulimba Cup, offers some advice to the young full-back Frank Drake of Toowoomba.**

his broken left arm hanging by his side. Souths had to win that game, as they did their last 11 games in a row - all sudden death showdowns - to achieve what went down in Aussie folklore as the *"Red and green miracle."* Later in his career, Clive Churchill moved to Brisbane where he was appointed captain-coach of the Northern Suburbs team in 1959. Not only did Churchill lead Norths to their first Brisbane premiership since 1940, he also revitalised the Queensland game by coaching the state side to a 3-1 series win over New South Wales after nine consecutive years of defeat. He also played full-back for Queensland and in the same year coached the

Sydney Grand Finals
1950 - Souths 21, beat Wests 15. ** *Att. 32,373.*
1951 - Souths 42, beat Manly 14. *Att. 28,505.*
1952 - Wests 22, beat Souths 12. *Att. 41,000.*
1953 - Souths 31, beat St.George 12. ** *Att. 44,581.*
(Mandatory from 1954 onwards)
1954 - Souths 23, beat Newtown 14. *Att. 45,759.*
1955 - Souths 12, beat Newtown 11. *Att. 42,466.*
1956 - St.George 18, beat Balmain 12. *Att. 61,987.*
1957 - St.George 31, beat Manly 9. *Att. 54,399.*
1958 - St.George 20, beat Wests 9. *Att. 63,282.*
1959 - St.George 20, beat Manly 0. *Att. 49,457.*
(** *Denotes figures for Final - no Grand Final required.*)

(Above) **Harry Bath of St.George involved in the infamous brawl during the 1959 Grand Final against Manly, which saw him sent off with Rex Mossop.**

Australian team to a series win over New Zealand before going away with the 1959 Kangaroos.

Souths' five Premierships in six seasons was a precursor to the start of St.George's incredible run of eleven consecutive titles. Saints won their first in 1956, with much of their success put down to the knowledge gained in England by their captain, and later coach, Ken Kearney. The hooker had been a Rugby Union international, recruited by Leeds to play Rugby League in 1948 who - after a very successful time at Headingley - returned home to Australia in 1952, where he joined St.George. Kearney's skills in scrummaging and forward play put the Saints ahead of their rivals, and this was increased when Harry Bath returned from his long career at Warrington, to add further steel and footballing skills. Bath gained notoriety for his part in a wild brawl in the 1959 Grand Final against Manly-Warringah, in which he fought with Rex Mossop (another who had returned from England after learning the League game with Leigh.)

The Sydney competition - which throughout the 'fifties comprised of ten clubs: Balmain, Canterbury-Bankstown, Easts, Manly-Warringah, Newtown, Norths, Parramatta, Souths, St.George and Wests - first introduced the sytem of a mandatory Grand Final in 1954. Before that, the system had been that if a minor premier (league leader) was beaten in a semi-final or final, the club had the right of challenge. It meant that the team which had finished on top after all the preliminary rounds deserved two chances.

The Australian Rugby League celebrated its 50th anniversary by staging the World Cup in 1957; two years later, as the decade drew to a close, its greatest pioneer, Dally Messenger, *"The Master,"* passed away on 24th November 1959, at the age of 76.

(Above)
Ken Kearney, captain-coach of St.George, makes a victory speech after winning the J.J.Giltinan Shield with their 1957 Grand Final win over Manly. Sydney's Lord Mayor Harry Jensen looks on. It was the second of what was to become St.George's remarkable eleven successive titles.

(Above, left)
Johnny Raper, as a teenage star with Newtown, joined St.George in 1959 and became an 'immortal.'

Brisbane Grand Finals

1950 - Easts 14, beat Wests 10.
1951 - Souths 20, beat Easts 10.
1952 - Wests 15, beat Brothers 14.
1953 - Souths 21, beat Easts 4.
1954 - Wests 35, beat Brothers 18.
1955 - Fortitude Valley 17, beat Brothers 7.
1956 - Brothers 17, beat Wests 10.
1957 - Fortitude Valley 18, beat Brothers 17.
1958 - Brothers 22, beat Fortitude Valley 7.
1959 - Norths 24, beat Brothers 18.

The game in France

(*Above*)
Paul Barriere, the most prestigious of all Presidents of the French Rugby League, who led the game in its golden years of success from 1947 to 1955, and founded the World Cup.

T he golden decade for French Rugby League was from its post-war revival up to 1955 - a time of great adventure, international success, sensational tours to Australia, mighty club sides, big crowds and never-to-be-forgotten star players. On the back of all that, the second half of the 'fifties ensured the game in France was still strong, but perhaps without the magic it had enjoyed before.

At the helm of the golden age was the young President of the French Rugby League, Paul Barriere. A native of Esperaza in the *Aude,* Barriere had been a member of the *Resistance* during the war, and was only 27 years old when he was elected President of the Rugby League Federation in 1947. Alongside him was a strong lieutenant in Claude Devernois, a weathy industrialist from Roanne who had created a stellar team of stars at his home club before the war.

They presided over a League which had big clubs in major cities, as well as the heartland towns like Carcassonne, Albi, Perpignan and Villeneuve. Biggest of the city teams was Marseille, financed by Paul Ricard and able to draw big crowds to the Velodrome stadium. Toulouse Olympique were also there,

(*Above*) **Puig-Aubert and Elie Brousse, two stars of the 1951 tour, in the colours of Paris Celtic.**

but not a major force in the 'fifties, and Lyon became a star-studded rival for Marseille when Claude Devernois sensationally moved his Roanne team - lock, stock and barrel - to the nearby big city. A Paris club was also in the League, and it enjoyed a massive publicity boost in the aftermath of France's first Australian tour in 1951 when - under the banner of Paris Celtic - mega stars like Puig-Aubert and Elie Brousse were recruited by their determined President Maurice Tardy. During the 'fifties, international matches continued to be played in Paris at the prestigious *Parc des Princes.*

Puig-Aubert had made his name with Carcassonne as the *Canaris* had established themselves as France's most decorated club in the post-war years. Brousse, meanwhile, although also a native Catalan, had moved north after being signed by Monsieur Devernois to play for Roanne, and then Lyon. It was the talents of Carcassonne and Lyon, along with Marseille, which provided the backbone of the 1951 French team which was so successful on its adventure to Australia. It was Paul Barrier's greatest gamble to send that team as the first French side in either code to go to the southern hemisphere, but boy did it pay off! The city of Marseille had never witnessed scenes like it as the heroes

Championship Finals

1950 - Carcassonne 21, beat Marseille 7.
(*At Perpignan - Att. 18,000.*)
1951 - Lyon 15, beat X111 Catalan 10.
(*At Stade Chapou, Toulouse - Att. 21,933.*)
1952 - Carcassonne 14, beat Marseille 6.
(*At Stade Chapou, Toulouse - Att. 16,645.*)
1953 - Carcassonne 19, beat Lyon 12.
(*At Le Stadium, Toulouse - Att. 22,500.*)
1954 - Bordeaux 7, beat Marseille 4.
(*At Le Stadium, Toulouse - Att. 8,000.*)
1955 - Lyon 7, beat Carcassonne 6.
(*At Le Stadium, Toulouse - Att. 12,000.*)
1956 - Albi 13, beat Carcassonne 5.
(*At Le Stadium, Toulouse - Att. 15,850.*)
1957 - X111 Catalan 14, beat Avignon 9.
(*At Le Stadium, Toulouse - Att. 9,000.*)
1958 - Albi 8, beat Carcassonne 6.
(*At Le Stadium, Toulouse - Att. 16,163.*)
1959 - Villeneuve 24, beat Lezignan 16.
(*At Le Stadium, Toulouse - Att. 13,000.*)

(Left)
Marseille's six players from the famous 1951 French touring team, are welcomed back to the Velodrome with the trophies won in Australia. Left to right: Beraud (in civvies), Perez, Rinaldi, Andre, Merquey and Jean Dop (holding the Franco-Australia cup.

returned and were given a New York style ticker-tape procession through the streets. Whilst the French international team continued to be successful, the domestic Championship and Cup competitions were dominated by four clubs: Carcassonne, Marseille, Lyon and *X111 Catalan* of Perpignan. By 1953, the new stadium in Toulouse had opened and become the home of the Championship Final for the rest of the decade.

Paul Barriere's ambition for the game saw him pull all the stops out to stage the first World Cup in 1954, especially as France had won the unofficial "world champions" tag for the previous three years. The tournament was a great success, but how disappointed Barriere was to see France lose the Final by just four points - knowing that so much prestige and unprecedented political support would have been generated by giving the nation an official World Cup winner.

It came as a hammer blow to the game in France when Barriere resigned as President in May 1955, on the eve of their second tour to Australia. Claude Devernois took over as President, and the tour was still a success - led by Jackie Merquey and with Jean Dop returning to entertain the Aussie crowds just as he had done in 1951. By this time Merquey had left Marseille and moved to the blossoming Avignon club, who were becoming a new force in the French game. Merquey's Avignon team, which included the mighty winger Andre Savonne (nicknamed *"The Bison"*), never won a Championship, but they took part in four Cup Finals in the second half of the 'fifties, winning two.

As the end of the decade approached, and the game in France lacking some of the earlier sparkle which had made it so popular when the likes of Puig-Aubert, Jo Crespo and Jean Dop were in their pomp, Claude Devernois made big headlines by signing four high-profile Rugby Union internationals for the Roanne club he had returned to after the big city Lyon club had come to an end. Pierre *"Papillon"* Lacaze, Jean Barthe and Aldo Quaglio all quickly became League internationals against Australia in Paris in 1959 and, along with Claude Mantoulan, and all went on to serve the game well in the 'sixties.

(Above) In the colours of Avignon, Jackie Merquey, one star who spanned the whole decade and through all the changes in France.

Lord Derby Cup Finals

1950 - X111 Catalan 12, beat Lyon 5.
(At Carcassonne - Att. 13,500.)
1951 - Carcassonne 22, beat Lyon 10.
(At Marseille - Att. 23,000.)
1952 - Carcassonne 28, beat X111 Catalan 9.
(At Marseille - Att. 14,384.)
1953 - Lyon 9, beat Villeneuve 8.
(At Perpignan - Att. 12,200.)
1954 - Lyon 17, beat X111 Catalan 15.
(At Cavaillon - Att. 8,000.)
1955 - Avignon 18, beat Marseille 10.
(At Carpentras - Att. 11,600.)
1956 - Avignon 25, beat Bordeaux 15.
(At Perpignan - Att. 5,800.)
1957 - Marseille 11, beat X111 Catalan 0.
(At Carcassonne - Att. 16,633.)
1958 - Villeneuve 20, beat Avignon 8.
(At Perpignan - Att. 5,473.)
1959 - X111 Catalan 7, beat Avignon 0.
(At Carcassonne - Att. 11,000.)

The Amateur game

(Above)
The England Amateur Under-19s team in 1959, before beating France 13-8 at Wigan. The captain is Phil Kitchin of Kells, with Frank Foster, another future Test player, standing far right.

The annual international matches against France were the highlight for amateur Rugby League players during the 1950s, with both Open Age and Junior caps to be won. The Juniors were Under-19s, although in the early years of the decade, notably 1951 and 1952, the England team allowed the inclusion of players registered with professional clubs up to the age of 21. In the absence of any national cup, the "holy grail" of all amateurs clubs was to win through to the first round proper of the Rugby League Challenge Cup. To achieve that, they had to win through a long series of preliminary rounds. The number of places for amateur teams in the Cup varied, to fit in with the changing number of senior clubs during the 'fifties, and also as Welsh clubs Cardiff and Llanelly were given places in 1950 and 1951, respectively, whilst both were not senior clubs. The decade held no giant-killing acts by the amateurs, although Rylands Recs. of Warrington did manage to hold Whitehaven to a 9-9 draw in their home leg in 1952, after they had lost the away leg 16-0. The following is a list of all the amateur clubs who took part in the Challenge Cup first round proper thoughout the 'fifties:

1950 - Broughton Moor, Worsley Boys' Club. **1951** - Broughton Moor, Latchford Albion. **1952** - Rylands Recs. **1953** - Orford Tannery, National Dock Labour Board (Hull). **1954** - Latchford Albion, Wheldale Colliery. **1955** - Dewsbury Celtic. **1956** - Stanningley, Triangle Valve. **1957** - Wakefield Loco, Widnes St.Marie's. **1958** - Orford Tannery, Lock Lane. **1959** - Astley & Tyldesley Colliery, Kells.

Amateur Internationals
1950 - England 5, France 7. (*Leeds.*)
1951 - France 10, England 7. (*Rodez.*)
1952 - England 3, France 3. (*Manchester.*)
1953 - France 18, England 12. (*Perpignan.*)
1954 - England 23, France 0. (*Leeds.*)
1955 - France 15, England 12. (*Tarbes.*)
1956 - England 22, France 19. (*St.Helens.*)
1957 - France 32, England 23. (*Tonneins.*)
1958 - England 14, France 24. (*Hull.*)
1959 - France 24, England 7. (*Villeneuve.*)
Totals from 10 matches played:
France 7 wins; England 2 wins; 1 draw.

Junior Internationals
1950 - France 17, England 0. (*Avignon.*)
1951 - England 23, France 7. (*Wigan.*)
1952 - France 8, England 5. (*Avignon.*)
1953 - England 9, France 13. (*Leigh.*)
1954 - France 2, England 13. (*Avignon.*)
1955 - England 36, France 2. (*Wigan.*)
1956 - France 8, England 10. (*Tarbes.*)
1957 - England 2, France 8. (*Oldham.*)
1958 - France 48, England 10. (*Limoux.*)
1959 - England 13, France 8. (*Wigan.*)
Totals from 10 matches played:
England 5 wins; France 5 wins.

(Above) The Shaw Cross boys' club team of Dewsbury in 1953 Left to right: (*Back row*): Mr. D. Hird (secretary), J.Farrar, M.Waring, B.Wilkinson, E.Wilson, D.Peace, Mr. F. Smith (chairman). (*Front row*): D. "Ginger" Smith, D. Smith, D.Moorhouse, H.Waring, A.Kilroy (captain), J.Smith, G.Bradshaw, C.Towler. Shaw Cross became one of Rugby League's most prolific talent nurseries with its most famous product in the 1950s being Mick Sullivan. On this 1953 team pictured, centre David Peace went on to be a foundation player at Blackpool Borough, whilst Austin Kilroy had a long career at Huddersfield.